The Architecture of Drama

PLOT, CHARACTER, THEME, GENRE, AND STYLE

David Letwin
Joe Stockdale
Robin Stockdale

The Scarecrow Press, Inc.
Lanham, Maryland • Toronto • Plymouth, UK
2008

SCARECROW PRESS, INC.

Published in the United States of America
by Scarecrow Press, Inc.
A wholly owned subsidiary of
The Rowman & Littlefield Publishing Group, Inc.
4501 Forbes Boulevard, Suite 200, Lanham, Maryland 20706
www.scarecrowpress.com

Estover Road
Plymouth PL6 7PY
United Kingdom

British Library Cataloguing in Publication Information Available

Library of Congress Cataloging-in-Publication Data
Letwin, David, 1960–
    The architecture of drama : plot, character, theme, genre, and style /
David Letwin, Joe Stockdale, and Robin Stockdale.
        p. cm.
    Includes bibliographical references and index.
    ISBN-13: 978-0-8108-6129-9 (pbk. : alk. paper)
    ISBN-10: 0-8108-6129-1 (pbk. : alk. paper)
    eISBN-13: 978-0-8108-6226-5
    eISBN-10: 0-8108-6226-3
    1. Drama—Technique. 2. Drama—History and criticism.—Theory, etc.
    I. Stockdale, Joe. II. Stockdale, Robin, 1925– III. Title.
    PN1661.L34 2008
    808.2—dc22

                                                    2008007537

⊚™The paper used in this publication meets the minimum requirements of
American National Standard for Information Sciences—Permanence of
Paper for Printed Library Materials, ANSI/NISO Z39.48-1992.
Manufactured in the United States of America.

Contents

Preface

This book is intended for practitioners of the dramatic arts who wish to master the craft of dramatic storytelling, for college professors teaching courses in dramatic literature who want to examine drama as something to be performed rather than merely read, and for lovers of theater and film who simply want deeper insight into what they are watching.

To this end, we make no great claims to groundbreaking scholarship or new theories of drama. We have synthesized the work of those who have gone before us, as well as our contemporaries, and filtered them through our own experiences as teachers, directors, writers, and actors. As with almost everything connected to the arts, the result is subjective, not scientific. We encourage the reader to critically examine our premises and conclusions as we have challenged the premises and conclusions of others.

The process of incorporating one's ideas with the ideas of others has predictable pitfalls. In the preface to his study of Chekhovian dramaturgy, *The Breaking String*, author Maurice Valency noted that the great observations of others fix themselves in our minds so indelibly that we often have trouble remembering they are not ours, and when integrating these insights into our own work, we may delude ourselves into what he called "a comforting sense of originality." Someone else—none of us can remember who—said that the penalty for a lifetime of reading is that you can't always remember whom to credit. In an attempt to redress any unintended oversight in this regard, we wish to acknowledge our debt to a broad range of artists, writers, and thinkers upon whose work this book is based.

Most of them are either mentioned in the body of the text or cited when appropriate. Among those who are not, we would like to acknowledge the influence of those who directly taught us, in particular Laura V. Shaw of Western Michigan University (and by extension those with whom she studied: Richard Boleslavsky, Maria Ouspenskaya, and Madam Dakahoniva of the American Laboratory Theatre), Walter Prichart Eaton, Preston H. Epps, Samuel Selden (whose major influence was Frederick Koch) of the University of North Carolina, and Campton Bell of the University of Denver. We would also like to acknowledge the influence of our colleagues from Purdue University, The School of the Arts at State University of New York at Purchase, the Mason Gross School of the Arts at Rutgers University, as well as countless discussions with fellow artists and students over the many years of our combined teaching and professional careers, along with special thanks to our colleague David Garfield, who in the past two years has answered our calls with "Garfield Reference"; friends and computer experts Elvin and Connie Clark of Tryon, North Carolina—he a whiz in a wide range of word processing programs, and she an actress with the eagle eyes of a hard-core English major junkie who focuses immediately on the errors we just happened to overlook; another valued friend Beverly Nichols, our first reader and critic. Thanks to Andrew Yoder, Production Editor of Scarecrow Press, and our boundless thanks to Stephen Ryan, Senior Editor of Arts and Literature, for his valuable and patient guidance throughout the publication process. Thanks to all.

Throughout this book we will be using *The Poetics of Aristotle*, translated by Preston H. Epps, because of its clarity and accessibility. Note that brackets [ ] in all quotations by Epps are his; all other bracketed material in this book is ours. Whenever we give a definition, it will be from either *American Heritage* (third edition) or *Webster's Collegiate* (fifth edition). Full references for the text boxes, along with numbered endnotes, are found at the end of each chapter. Since plays and screenplays are published in various anthologies, we will not cite publishers or page numbers.

It is impossible to write on any subject without exposing one's biases. To that end, we acknowledge that our focus reflects a conscious orientation toward Western drama, the drama with which we are overwhelmingly engaged and familiar. You will also note alternating tones in the writing with our use of formal and familiar English. This is a deliberate choice on our part. We feel we will better reach and therefore serve our targeted audience with such a juxtaposition rather than restricting ourselves to the usual uppercase academic tone.

One final point: we know how difficult it is to find a satisfactory solution to the pronoun/gender issue. No attempt at clever grammatical legerdemain can obscure the clunkiness of "s/he," "he or she," or making a plural so we can use "they" as if to universalize the sex of individuals. Therefore, we beg our readers' indulgence if we fall back on a slight variation of the convenient tradition and simply refer to everyone as "she."

*   *   *

Acknowledgment of Permissions

Excerpts of the following works are used by permission of:

The Poetics of Aristotle translated by Preston H. Epps. Copyright © 1942 by the University of North Carolina Press, renewed in 1970 by Preston H. Epps. Used by permission of the publisher.

A Portrait of a Madonna by Tennessee Williams from *27 Wagons Full of Cotton*. Copyright © 1945 by The University of the South. Reprinted by permission of New Directions Publishing Corp.

A Streetcar Named Desire by Tennessee Williams. Copyright © 1947 by The University of the South. Reprinted by permission of New Directions Publishing Corp.

Camino Real by Tennessee Williams. Copyright © 1953 as "Camino Real," revised and published version, by The University of the South, renewed in 1981 by The University of the South. Reprinted by permission of New Directions Publishing Corp.

Death of a Salesman by Arthur Miller. Copyright © 1949, renewed in 1977 by Arthur Miller. Reprinted by permission of Viking Penguin, a division of Penguin Group (USA) Inc.

Betrayal by Harold Pinter. Copyright © 1978 by H. Pinter Ltd. Reprinted by permission of Grove/Atlantic, Inc.

Boy's Life by Howard Korder from *Boy's Life and Other Plays*. Copyright © 1989 by Howard Korder. Reprinted by permission of Grove/Atlantic, Inc.

Prologue

What happened? What the hell happened?!

—Jake Holman, *The Sand Pebbles*

Human beings, it would seem, have an almost genetic predisposition toward dramatic storytelling. From the theater festivals of ancient Athens to a Broadway musical, from Balinese trance dances to Hollywood melodramas, from Japanese Kabuki theater to a Punch and Judy puppet show, most cultures lay claim to a dramatic tradition of one kind or another.

What explains this fascination? Why, across time and place, do we see so rich and varied a legacy of dramatic presentations?

Some of the answers are straightforward enough. People seek diversion in life, and drama can certainly provide that. We go to a theater or a movie house, the lights dim, and for two or three hours we are able to lose ourselves in an imaginary world, freed—if only momentarily—from our own troubles and mundane concerns. We also take pleasure in the sheer visual or aural spectacle of drama: the costumes, special effects, scenery, photography, music, and language. Indeed, we often remember the stunning cinematography of a film or the helicopter landing onstage more than we do the story itself. Aristotle, back in the fourth century B.C.E., was on to something even more basic. Humans, he noted, are naturally drawn to artistically accurate imitations of what they see around them. Hard to argue with that. Have you ever met anyone who doesn't enjoy a bang-on impersonation of a friend or celebrity?

Yet these observations, true as they are, ignore the deeper source of drama's hold over us. We turn to drama, as we do to all the story arts, because at its best it satisfies a powerful desire to find meaning and order in a world that can often appear senseless and chaotic.

This craving for coherence can be seen all around us. People everywhere seem to respond restlessly to a life in which the causal links that tie events together are unapparent, broken, or nonexistent. Imagine coming home one day and finding, say, the lock on your front door moved from the right side to the left. No big deal, right? What's a few inches? The key still fits; the door still locks. Compared to problems of global warming or world hunger, this would hardly seem worth mentioning. Yet think how frantically your mind would scroll through every conceivable explanation for this bizarre, if minor, reordering of reality. And can you imagine the near total psychic collapse you would suffer if you failed to find one? The rising panic as you wondered whether you were absolutely losing your mind?

Why would you react this way? Because you—like most of us—don't like it when life doesn't make sense. From a toddler's obsessive fascination with the sound of its rattle, to a physicist's life-long search for the unified field theory, we spend our lives relentlessly sorting through the raw, unordered experience of life, trying to shape it into a knowable form. In short, humans have a passionate need to say, "Ah, I get it!"

The search for clarity, however, can prove frustratingly elusive. Learning that a toy makes noise when we shake it is one thing, making the deeper existential connections of life is quite another. What does it all mean? How did that happen? Why do I feel this way? These questions are always with us, if not always consciously, then certainly just below the surface. We search for answers, but we're too close to the puzzle of life to see how all the pieces fit together. It is as if we were a speck of paint on Michelangelo's fresco on the ceiling of the Sistine Chapel. We go about our daily job, filling that space until one day, weary and disgruntled, we ask, "What the hell am I doing?" Even if we are told that we fill a small but important part in the hand of God reaching out to man, the explanation is unreal because we cannot see our function, let alone see it in relationship to the whole. So one day we just flake off and float to the chapel floor. Looking up, we see that infinitesimally small space that is now empty—a space that we once filled. "Ahhh," we say, "Now I see. Now, I understand!"

"Ahhh, I see!" is an audience's response to a performance of a story in dramatic form. Dramas provide us that crucial distancing we need to see life's painting in its entirety. From the tenth row of the orchestra or from our couch in front of the television, we can see the relationship between action and consequence, cause and effect, anarchy and order. Watching these relationships come to life is an immensely satisfying and entertaining experience. There is nothing surprising about this. As Aristotle observed, learning is the most enjoyable human activity.

And what does it mean to learn, if not to complete the journey from chaos to coherence, from confusion to clarity, from "What the hell happened?" to "Ah, I get it!"?

Of course, the same general observations could be made of other storytelling forms: news reports, novels, and poetry, for example. These, too, can help us move from chaos to order. How does drama differ from these

---

LEARNING IS THE MOST PLEASANT OF ALL EXPERIENCES

Two causes, and natural ones too, seem generally responsible for the rise of the art of poetry: (1) the natural desire to imitate, which is present from childhood and differentiates man as the most imitative of all living creatures as well as enables him to gain his earliest knowledge through imitation, and (2) universal enjoyment in imitations. We find an indication of this in experience: for we view with pleasure reproductions of objects which in real life it pains us to look upon—likenesses of very loathsome animals or dead bodies, for instance. This is especially true if the reproductions are executed with unusual accuracy. The reason for this is that learning is the most pleasant of all experiences, not only for philosophers but for the rest of mankind as well, although mankind has but a small share in this experience. In fact, mankind's pleasure in beholding likenesses of objects is due to this: as they contemplate reproductions of objects they find themselves gaining knowledge as they try to reason out what each thing is; for instance, that this man is such and such a person. Of course, if the spectator happens never to have seen the object which is depicted, the pleasure he experiences will not be due to the reproduction as such, but to the workmanship, or the color, or some similar reason.

Aristotle, *The Poetics of Aristotle*, trans. Preston H. Epps (Chapel Hill: The University of North Carolina Press, 1942), 5–6.

forms? The best place to start is to make clear what we mean by the word *drama* in the first place. With the caveat that exceptions to this definition abound—in fact, you will find exceptions to almost everything we say in this book—drama, for our purposes, can be taken to mean stories of human beings in conflict, performed through action for an audience, either live, over the radio, or on screen.

That drama involves action is clear from the etymology of the word itself. It comes from the ancient Greek *dran*, meaning to do or to act. Unlike a novel, or the nightly news, or a telephone conversation in which you describe a problem to your mother, dramas are stories performed through *action* rather than explained through *narration*. This action, moreover, is taking place *now*, in what playwright Thornton Wilder called "the perpetual present time,"[1] rather than in the past, as is typically the case when a story is narrated.

Some will be quick to point out that dramas have been written in which animals, gods, and even objects have played the leading roles. This is an illusion. They may outwardly *look* like those other things, but they speak, think, behave, and essentially *are* human beings. Even documentaries on the animal kingdom—which can no doubt be very dramatic— still anthropomorphize the animals in such a way as to make their stories comprehensible to us.

That conflict is also central to the idea of drama is obvious by the way the term is used in daily life. When we describe an episode from life as being dramatic, we are almost always referring to the heightened level of conflict occurring between the participants. While it is entirely possible to write poetry or tell a story without focusing on conflict, it is safe to say that most people would regard a play or film without any recognizable conflict as essentially undramatic.

The reasons for the inseparable connection between drama and conflict are twofold. First, conflict is extremely compelling. Does an argument between a couple on a crowded street corner ever lack an audience? On the contrary, such eruptions always and immediately attract a crowd of interested observers. Dramas need interested observers as well, and whatever else a drama seeks to achieve, it will fail if it doesn't provide the audience with enough conflict to hold its attention.

Second, life is essentially an ongoing conflict between what we want and what is stopping us from getting it. To enter a room, you must get through the door; to ask for a date, you must confront your fear of rejection; to win the World Championship of Poker, you must beat several thousand other players who want to win as badly as you. Very little in life comes without a struggle of some kind, and any drama that lacks struggle will not only seem boring but fundamentally false.

Dramatic stories also require an audience. People dance and sing by and for themselves. Painters and writers paint and write in solitude, and although they may well dream of gallery openings and bestseller lists, their art isn't considered unfinished because it is never seen by anyone else. But a play or a screenplay is just a manuscript sitting on a desk until it has an audience.

How does drama convey a coherent picture of life to an audience, and orchestrate conflict in such a way that those watching feel engaged and ultimately satisfied?

Through its architecture.

Architecture, by both connotation and definition, is the art and science, style and method, of designing and creating something. Most commonly, that something is thought of as a building, but it can be—indeed is—defined as any created form, such as a system of government, a symphonic composition, or, in our case, the production of a film or stage play. By using this word in the title of our book, we are implicitly acknowledging that drama *has* method, that there *is* a design to its creation—what writer Eric Kahler described as an "inner organizational coherence"[2]—and that these methods and designs can be studied and apprehended.

Any study of architecture in the arts must also concern itself not just with structure and design, but also, and more fundamentally, with aesthetics, that branch of philosophy that deals with the nature of beauty and our response to it. This connection is unavoidable for anyone truly passionate about art and its centrality to the human experience.

In these cynical times, however, it often seems unfashionable to speak of beauty as an end in itself, almost as if it's something to be embarrassed about. Our culture is driven by material acquisitions, monetary wealth and success, not by such effete pursuits as aesthetics. After all, only a flaky romantic would get all warm and fuzzy inside by walking across the Brooklyn Bridge on a clear winter's night, gazing up in wonder at its gothic piers rising like cathedrals out of the East River, its span of cables like harp strings, taking in the panorama of light, steel, and glass on the far shore, right?

Wrong.

The beauty of that bridge, and the spirit of creative invention it represents, should move *anyone* with the slightest sensitivity. It stands as a testament to human achievement greater than anything Wall Street, Madison Avenue, or Sony Electronics has ever, or will ever, produce. And what separates it from all the bridges built across time isn't its engineering or its function; in fact, it's no better at getting people across a river than any other bridge. What places it near the top of iconic American images is its beauty, period.

But what is beauty? The dictionary defines it as "a delightful quality associated with harmony of form or color, excellence of craftsmanship, truthfulness, originality ... a quality or feature that is most effective, gratifying or telling ... an outstanding example." These are hard definitions to pin down. In "Ode on a Grecian Urn," John Keats may have said it better: "Beauty is truth, truth beauty,—that is all / Ye know on earth, and all ye need to know."[3] One thing we know for sure is that both beauty and truth are in the mind of the beholder. So, have you beheld it? You may have experienced beauty in nature, but art is not nature. It is an imitation of nature, and therefore once removed from it. It is also the product of a conscious, human, creative act, unlike a tree, or a lake, or a sunset.

What experience of artistic beauty and truth do you have? That is what we are talking about. What did the Rockefeller Panel Report members mean when they wrote, "the arts are not for a privileged few but for the many, that their place is not on the periphery of society but at its center, that they are not just a form of recreation but are of central importance to our well being and happiness."[4] And—although we could not find it in her over 800-page autobiography, *Living My Life*—myth has it, Emma Goldman told her Communist compatriots, "If I can't dance, I don't want to be a part of your revolution."

We can't speak for everyone, but we can give our examples of artistic beauty experienced: Michelangelo's *David* in the gallery of The Academy in Florence; a late August night with a full moon in Agra, India, viewing— through the frame of an arch in the surrounding wall—the whole of the Taj Mahal; James Agee's novel *A Death in the Family*; Gabriel Axel's film *Babette's Feast*; The Beatles' song "Strawberry Fields Forever"; and how about the overture to the musical *Gypsy*? The work of art need not be famous: in a small museum in Piacenza, Italy, with mostly indifferent art, an ancient painting depicts a soldier going to war. A woman, assumed to be his wife or lover, has thrown her arms around him and his right hand— turned palm up and slightly elevated—is in a "I must go, what else can I do?" gesture that brings sudden tears to the viewer by its truth. In all of these instances, the beauty perceived comes through a multitude of sensory and intellectual impressions, which are achieved through the work's architectural components that, united, form the whole of the piece.

For Aristotle, "beauty consists in magnitude and arrangement" of the plot, which he called "the soul of drama."[5] But he also recognized that there was much more to a drama than just "a beginning, middle and end" or "proper magnitude" of its plot.[6] In *Poetics*, he addressed such matters as the definition of character, their qualities and ways of being portrayed; causes for the rise of dramatic storytelling and its relationship to a view of life; the effect tragedy (and, by inference, any kind of story) has on an audience; and the mode or manner of diction. He was concerned with all these matters— all related to the architecture of dramatic storytelling. More importantly, he implicitly recognized the interdependence of these components and their vital relationship to the whole.

Building on his insights, as well as the insights of those who came after him, we believe the architecture of drama—that which produces its inner organizational coherence, and by extension its beauty and truth— can be expressed by and examined through five discrete component parts: plot, character, theme, genre, and style.

Plot

By plot, we mean the seven structural components used in the selection and arrangement of events in the story. No drama can possibly contain all the events that could conceivably relate to the story. It would go on for days, weeks, years, or lifetimes. A writer must select, from the infinite number of possibilities, only those particular events that illustrate the meaning of the story, produce the desired response in the audience, and can be comprehended within a couple of hours or so.

These selected events are then typically arranged in some pattern that is both coherent and interesting. Simply throwing events randomly together, with no concern for order or dramatic effect, will, more often than not, fail to satisfy the audience. It will resemble too much the way things appear to us in real life, and we are unlikely to spend our money, time, and energy watching something formless.

Character

Character not only means the individuals who are in the drama, but it also, and more importantly, refers to the true essence of those individuals—their character—which can only be revealed through the actions they take over the course of the story. Want to discover the truth of someone? Put her in a situation in which she must make a really difficult choice and then watch what happens. Everything—age, gender, weight, nationality, value system, favorite breakfast cereal (all those traits that we collectively refer to as characteristics)—pale in importance compared to what a person does when the heat is on. In this regard, one of the main functions of the plot is to turn up that heat as much as possible. The hotter the fire, the more one's true character is revealed.

Theme

Theme in this context does *not* mean the subject matter of the story. Theme is the artist's point of view on the subject matter. If plot answers the question "What's happening?" theme answers the question "What does it mean?" The plot of the film *Jaws* at its most literal concerns the struggle between humans and a twenty-five-foot shark. The theme is how writer Peter Benchley, director Steven Spielberg, and all the other artists working on the film viewed that struggle and what they think it tells us about human existence. Even the most action-filled plots and interesting characters will go for nothing if they ultimately do not serve that larger point.

Genre

By genre, we mean the type of drama being presented, these types being differentiated primarily by the response they elicit in the people watching. When you go to the video store, the DVDs are arranged by these genres—comedy, horror, romance, etc.—so that you can make an educated guess as to the response any particular film is likely to produce in you, and pick accordingly. If you want to scream in shock and grab the person you're sitting next to, you don't pick up the romantic comedy *When Harry Met Sally*; if you want to drink warm cocoa and weep through a box of Kleenex, you don't rent *The Exorcist*. Artists are—or should be—as aware of this as you are.

Style

Finally, every drama has a style, a distinctive or characteristic mode of expression, that is manifest in the author's writing as well as the way the story is performed. Just as curved lines and tail fins are characteristic of American cars in the 1950s, so iambic pentameter verse, the use of metaphor, and a relatively empty stage are characteristic of both the way Shakespeare wrote his plays as well as the way they were performed in his day. Note that Shakespeare's style is not a product of any particular plot, theme, or genre; it applies as much to *Hamlet* as it does to *Merry Wives of Windsor*.

In examining the five components of dramatic storytelling's architecture, along with their subheadings, we admit up front that a divide-and-conquer strategy has its pitfalls. We are attempting to break into independent parts things which, by their very nature, are interrelated. Can you really talk about plot without addressing character? Actions of the characters can only be taken within the events that have been selected. How can you study them separately? It's like trying to separate the heart and the lungs. The heart can't pump without oxygenated blood, and the lungs can't process oxygen without blood pumped from the heart.

Yet when you have a heart attack or a ruptured lung, you want a specialist, not a general practitioner. We intend to use the same approach in analyzing the architecture of dramatic storytelling as a whole. For example, in the first of the five chapters—"Plot"—we will focus on each of the seven parts that give a plot its internal structural coherence, while at the same time showing how these seven parts are interrelated and organically connected to a drama's structure as a whole. Sometimes it's messy, but when you get right down to the arts, everything is.

Although we are examining this architecture as it applies to the dramatic form, these components are deeply rooted in the way any of us would normally convey even the simplest story. Imagine, for example, that you want to tell your friends how you fell flat on your face at your tango lesson. For months, you have been dying to dance with that beautiful woman in red. One night, as luck would have it, you end up as partners. You finally get your chance to impress her with your *gancho* and *cadencia* (we don't know what those words mean either, but apparently you do them when you tango). So far, so good. But just as you go for your *caminando valsiado*—splat!—down you go. Everyone laughs at you. Your pants split down the backside. The woman in red, mortified, scurries away into the arms of a more accomplished dancer. And at the insistence of the instructor, a seventy-year-old balding male with roving hands and bad breath, you spend the rest of the evening—your back to the wall, naturally—with him as a partner practicing your *caminando valsiado*!

Without any conscious thought to the story's overall architecture or the plot's structure, you instinctively know that you would not include a lengthy and detailed description of the breakfast you ate the morning of the class, or how you mowed the lawn afterward, or the flock of birds that flew overhead on your way to the studio. Those events are simply irrelevant to the story. We all know what it is like to listen to someone who lacks this sense of selectivity, telling us every detail and event with no regard to its importance. When trapped with a person like that, how long does it take before you start sneaking looks at your watch? But you also wouldn't begin such a story with the line, "and just as I went for my *caminando valsiado*— splat!—down I went," followed by, "She was wearing a red dress," concluding with "Just as I was going into my third *arrastre.*" First of all, no one would understand what you were talking about. Second, we tend to arrange events so that the most exciting things come toward the end, rather than at the beginning. If you put your grand finale at the start of the story, why should we stick around for the rest of it?

Would you feed us a steady stream of insignificant data regarding your height and weight? Or your hair color? Or your partner's Episcopalian beliefs? Not if you want to keep us interested, you wouldn't. Instead you'd focus on the actions of the story, and what they ultimately reveal about you and your partner's character. You try to execute the tango equivalent of a triple somersault in front of the whole class. In a situation where the pressure is high, you make a tough choice. What does that tell us about you? You're brave? Foolhardy? Starved for attention? As a result, your partner chose to dump you and find someone else. What does that say about her? She's snobby? Insecure? A perfectionist?

Whatever is revealed, the story ultimately serves to express your theme, or point of view of life. It might be "Overconfidence leads to rejection," or "We don't get what we want when we try too hard," or even "It's better to risk humiliation than to play it safe." You may have so internalized the meaning of your story that you are unable to articulate it. However, the selection of events and the actions of the characters in some way must illustrate and illuminate a theme, or they wouldn't be in your story in the first place.

From the very second you begin the story, you also have in your mind an idea of how you would like your audience to respond. Maybe you want people to laugh at your folly. Or maybe you want them to pity your humiliation. If the former, you reenact your tumble, in all its clumsy glory; if the latter, you quietly, simply describe how it felt to see your partner put her arms around someone else. You don't think about the genre. You don't have to. Consciously or not, you just naturally do what it takes to get your audience to react the way you would like.

Finally, you have a style in telling the story that is characteristic of you. Your gestures, choice of words, facial expressions, they are a part of that style. It's organic to you. If for no discernible reason you suddenly started speaking in verse, or using the words thee and thou, or stuck your hand inside your shirt placket like Napoleon and struck a series of statuesque poses, it would seem strange. Your audience would probably start trading glances. Why? It's just not characteristic of the way you express yourself. And while we're at it, what of the tango itself? To say it's a dance does nothing to distinguish it from hip hop, the rumba, or the waltz, which are also types of dance. What separates the tango from others is that it is executed in a different way that is characteristic of it alone; it has, in short, a different style.

We mentioned above that the architectural components of dramatic storytelling are not always employed consciously. We've spent a lifetime telling stories. Most of us have internalized how to do it, although some clearly do it better than others. But there is a difference between a five-minute story shared among friends and a two-hour drama for an audience of strangers. Those audiences bring with them expectations that far exceed those of your pals. If you were to try to turn your tango incident into a short film or a one-act play, you might discover that your instincts and inspiration—in short, your raw talent—won't be sufficient to satisfy those expectations.

Don't get us wrong: all art starts with the heart and the guts. Without that, all you get are lifeless clichés and pale imitations. But something more is required. That something is craft. As writer Robert McKee notes, "Talent without craft is like fuel without an engine. It burns wildly but accomplishes nothing."[7] In this case, that craft is the knowledge of the basic parts of drama's architecture and how they fit together. Except for a lucky few with God-given inspiration, this knowledge is acquired through study and analysis as much as through intuition.

Insights gained from a study of dramatic storytelling's architecture should prove as useful as a tool that exploits the artist's work to its fullest potential and shapes it into the most powerful dramatic production possible. Yet we know that the creative process is not uniform. Some—especially writers—may shy away from an analysis, fearing it will throttle their creativity. If you truly feel a conscious study of drama's architecture will rob you of your impulses and your talent, then by all means go with your instincts. Your audience, not a book, will ultimately judge the wisdom of your choice.

It is also important to acknowledge that, for many practitioners, analytical inquiry is not what they reject. They simply disagree with the more fundamental premises upon which this book is based.

For some, the performer, not the story, is at the heart of the dramatic experience. In this view, stories are simply one aspect of drama, not its defining characteristic. For others, drama is not necessarily about the transmission of coherent ideas or points of view. Over the past century or so, practitioners from Antonin Artaud to Jerzy Grotowski to Richard Foreman to modern-day performance artists have seen and continue to see drama as rooted in and expressive of the subconscious; something to be experienced through sounds, gestures, and images rather than understood through any rational architectural and structural devices. Indeed, many of these artists feel that such traditional dramatic terms as plot, character, theme, genre, and style—even language itself—are no longer relevant to a fractured world without shared beliefs or reference points.

The following is the entire dialogue of the play *To Understand Weeping*, written by the Italian futurist Giacomo Balla in 1916:

Man Dressed in Black: To understand weeping …

Man Dressed in White: mispicchirtitotiti

Man Dressed in Black: 48

Man Dressed in White: brancapatarsa

Man Dressed in Black: 1215 but mi …

Man Dressed in White: ullurbusssssut

Man Dressed in Black: 1 it seems like you are laughing

Man Dressed in White: sgnacarsnaipir

Man Dressed in Black: 111.111.011 I forbid you to laugh

Man Dressed in White: parplecurplototplaplint

Man Dressed in Black: 888 but for G-o-d-s sake don't laugh!

Man Dressed in White: iiiiiirrrrririrriri

Man Dressed in Black: 1234 Enough! Stop it! Stop laughing.

Man Dressed in White: I must laugh.

Curtain[8]

Like it or hate it, it's hard to recognize the architectural components and structural parts we have been and will be discussing. The selection and arrangement of events appears random. It's not clear who the characters are or what they are discussing, much less what is revealed about them. What it all means or how we are expected to respond is anybody's guess.

Whatever label you apply to perspectives such as these—modernism, postmodernism, deconstructionism, New Wave, theater of images, to name a few—they tend to unite around one governing idea: life cannot be understood by the conscious mind, and any attempt to make life's experience conform to coherent architectural principles will inevitably produce false art.

We come to praise these perspectives, not to bury them. New ideas are the lifeblood of all art. Honest challenges to accepted convention are vital. Artists who genuinely feel that life defies any logic whatsoever are duty-bound to express such a view through their art. Anything less, indeed, would be dishonest on their part—and dishonesty is the worst sin an artist can commit. Some practitioners of film and theater have twisted the architectural components we will discuss out of all recognition and reconfigured them in provocative and startling new ways. Many of these artists have devoted—if comparatively small—followings the world over. And that is exactly as it should be. It is ultimately up to audiences to engage the iconoclasts and determine for themselves whether or not their work has the ring of truth.

Their work. Meaning, work they themselves have written. A whole set of other issues arise when interpretive dramatic artists deliberately try to create chaos and incoherence out of someone else's writing that had, or has, no such intention. We will discuss the so-called director's vision later in the book. For now, let us simply note that having Lear enter on a tricycle or Hamlet speak his lines backward is, to put it mildly, not without its risks.

Whatever one may feel about recent approaches to writing and interpreting drama, this much is certain: the architectural components discussed in this book have an unassailable pedigree. They go back more than 2,500 years. New and revolutionary theories always force a restoration, or at the very least a re-examination, of what has stood the test of time. Dramatic storytelling that seeks to express a coherent view of life has passed that test. It has been overwhelmingly popular with audiences throughout history and around the world, and continues to be so today.

In Act 3 of Sam Shepard's play *Buried Child*, Vince describes his reaction to seeing his reflection in the glass of his car, as he drives late at night:

> I could see myself in the windshield. My face. My eyes. I studied my face. Studied everything about it. As though I was looking at another man. As though I could see his whole race behind him. Like a mummie's face. I saw him dead and alive at the same time. In the same breath. In the windshield, I watched him breathe as though he was frozen in time. And every breath marked him. Marked him forever without him knowing. And then his face changed. His face became his father's face. Same bones. Same eyes. Same nose. Same breath. And his father's face changed to his Grandfather's face. And it went on like that. Changing. Clear on back to faces I'd never seen before but still recognized. Still recognized the bones underneath. The eyes. The breath. The mouth.

Although an individual unique to his own time and place, when Vince looks closely at his reflection, he sees the same bones, eyes, nose, mouth—the same structures—as are in the faces of his ancestors. The same is true of dramas created today and their relationship to the architecture of dramatic storytelling that has been, and will be, used to satisfy humankind's unending search for understanding, for the answer to that eternal question: What the hell happened?

Notes

1. Thornton Wilder, "Some Thoughts on Playwriting," in *The Intent of the Artist*, ed. Augusto Centeno (New York: Russell & Russell, 1941), 83.

2. Erich Kahler, *The Disintegration of Form in the Arts* (New York: George Braziller, Inc., 1967), 4.

3. John Keats, "Ode on a Grecian Urn," stanza 5.

4. Rockefeller Panel Report, *The Performing Arts, Problems and Prospects* (New York: McGraw-Hill Book Company, 1965), 11.

5. Aristotle, *Poetics*, 16 and 14.

6. Aristotle, *Poetics*, 15 and 16.

7. Robert McKee, *Story: Substance, Structure, Style and The Principles of Screenwriting* (London: Methuen Publishing Ltd., 1999), 28.

8. Mira Felner and Claudia Orenstein, *The World of Theatre*, which includes Giacomo Balla's *To Understand Weeping* (New York: Pearson Education, Inc., 2006), 160.

Plot

Ask ten people to describe the plot of William Shakespeare's *Macbeth*, and you would probably get some variation on the following: A Scottish nobleman and his wife hatch a plan to kill their king so the nobleman can take over the throne. After a brief but intense struggle with both his conscience and his wife, he commits the murder and seizes the crown. However, others loyal to the dead king fight against this usurpation. At the story's end, these loyalists kill the ambitious nobleman and restore the crown to the murdered king's rightful heir.

Ask ten other people to recount the plot of the film *The Wizard of Oz*[1] and you would probably hear something like this: A young girl is swept off a Kansas farm by a tornado and deposited in the magical world of Oz. Desperate to return home, she ventures down a yellow brick road to seek the help of a powerful wizard. After confronting talking trees, flying monkeys, a wicked witch, and the wizard himself, she gets her wish and is delivered back to the safety of her Kansas homestead.

The architectural components of each of these dramas are completely different. Yet they are arranged around the same seven structural parts of plot that are found in many dramas the world over. These parts are:

Leading Character—The central person in the plot.
The Inciting Incident—The event that throws the leading character out of balance.
Objective—The goal the leading character seeks to restore the balance of her life.
Obstacle—That force, or forces, preventing the leading character from reaching her goal.

The Crisis—The toughest—and usually final—decision made by the leading character to overcome the obstacles.

The Climax—The final showdown with the obstacles that arise out of the crisis, during which the leading character either gains or fails to gain her objective.

The Resolution—The new balance that is created as a result of the climax.

These seven structural parts are so fundamental to dramatic story-telling that we hardly even notice their presence, let alone reflect on their purpose. There is nothing either theoretical or contrived about them, for they reflect the rhythm of life as human beings experience it. The truth is, most of us encounter these elements so often that we already know exactly what they are; we just haven't thought about them in terms of drama. It might be helpful to visualize these seven parts unfolding in the following way.

Many terms have been given to describe this form, or shape, of drama: Aristotelian, linear, climactic, classical, to name a few. Whatever you call it, this form weaves these parts of structure into a tight, cause-and-effect story that builds in intensity to a strong climactic ending with a detectable change in fortune for the leading character. It typically stresses the "inner organizational coherence" of these parts, and tends to focus on a main plot with, at most, a couple of leading characters.

A description of the characteristics of this plot structure doesn't begin to convey the breadth, depth, and variety of dramas that have used it. It is found the world over, although it is most identified with the Western dramatic tradition. Its ubiquity speaks to its popularity with audiences, and a list of dramatists that have to one degree or another worked in this form stretches from Sophocles and Shakespeare to Kurosawa and Scorsese.

But this should not obscure the fact that other plot forms have also emerged that not only deviate from this form but also reject it altogether. Before we examine these seven parts in detail, though, we feel it is important to quickly examine some of the more signal departures. You may have no acquaintance with the examples cited. But that in itself should tell you something: that in the evolutionary process of artistic forms, some do not survive, or they survive only in part by influencing and enhancing the fittest that do survive.

Working backward, from the present to the past, the shape of Eugene Ionesco's *The Bald Soprano*, written in 1950, is a circle. Its inner organizational arrangement is that it curves back around to where it started rather than building up to a rousing climax and clear resolution. It presents life as a cycle with no beginning, middle, or end. Events do not proceed in succession according to probability and necessity, which eliminates cause-and-effect reasoning. That's the point. The cyclical plot represents the absurdist view of life. The play opens with Mrs. Smith's line, "There it's nine o'clock. We've drunk the soup, and eaten the fish and chips." After several episodes that bear no causal relationship to one another, the lights come up on dinner guests Mr. and Mrs. Martin, who, like the Smiths, are seated at the table, and Mrs. Martin says the same line as Mrs. Smith said at the play's beginning.[2]

One would be hard-pressed to locate any of the seven structural parts of plot in such a play. In fact, so thoroughly did this play break with these elements that Ionesco subtitled it an "anti-play." Most of us, of course, aren't looking for anti-plays, and that may explain why this plot has more or less come and gone with little if any discernible influence on the major surviving plots.

An earlier departure from the classical plot structure is sometimes referred to as the "dream form," from August Strindberg's *The Dream Play* written in 1900, a year after Freud's *Interpretation of Dreams*, which isn't to suggest any relationship other than the spirit of the times. In the preface, Strindberg explains the form:

> [I] tried to imitate the disconnected but apparently logical form of a dream. . . . everything is possible and likely. Time and space do not exist; on an insignificant basis of reality the imagination spins and weaves new patterns: a blending of memories, experiences, free inventions, absurdities, and improvisations. The characters split, double, redouble, evaporate, condense, scatter, and converge.[3]

The paradox seems to be "disconnected but apparent logical form," and would appear to rest upon and be unified by a single subconscious point of view of the leading character. But that can become problematic, so subjective as not to convey any rational connection at all. Harold Taylor in his essay, "Art and Intellect," comments:

> The unconscious . . . is often confused with creative imagination. I would like to say one or two things about the unconscious and about the stream of consciousness in the work of the artist. I ask, "The stream of whose consciousness?" Some people's unconscious is a great dull area with some obvious things in it, which we all have, but everyone's unconscious is not equally interesting. The mere exposure of the unconscious does no honor to art.[4]

More so than the circular plot, this form has influenced and merged with more traditional plots structures, particularly in its use of nonsequential time. It goes backward and forward—as in a dream—and may represent both past and present time in the same scene simultaneously, as in the card-playing scene with Willy and his next-door neighbor Charley in *Death of a Salesman*. Or present and past time may be shown in films through the use of interlinear cuts via flashback to reveal linkage in cause and effect. It is the freedom from the restraints of sequential time that is the dream form's great contribution, as it gives a cinematic fluidity to storytelling and eliminates exposition.

A third plot is the "episodic." The term *episodic* has several different meanings regarding a plot's structure. The great Elizabethan and Spanish Golden Age playwrights are often said to have written episodic dramas because their plots extended over a period of time that did not conform to Aristotle's "one revolution of the sun or depart only slightly from that rule."[5] They used lots of locations and characters and had multiple plot lines with many scenes or episodes. This form of drama was itself a product of the earlier medieval theater, which used this structure to act out biblical stories for parishioners who were either illiterate or did not understand Latin.

But by this term, we are referring to a more specific distinction first made by Aristotle in his *Poetics*. By an "episodic plot," Aristotle wrote, "I mean one in which the episodes are not arranged according to the law of probability and necessity."[6] In other words, an episodic plot is one that does not stress cause-and-effect linkage between the events of the story.

Bertold Brecht's *Mother Courage and Her Children* is an example of such a plot. The play has twelve scenes, the first starting in Dalarna in 1624, followed by other scenes in different times and places covering the Thirty Years War. Some of these scenes—for example, where the title character sings "The Song of the Great Capitulation"—stand alone, unrelated in plot to its previous or following scene; some scenes—such as the death of Kattrin—could be played as a one-act play. Most of the episodes, in their internal organization, do, in fact, contain all of the seven parts of plot mentioned at the beginning of this chapter, but most scenes do not necessarily relate to the scene that came before or after.

Since Aristotle observed that "anything whose presence or absence is no discernible difference is no essential part of the whole,"[7] he did not think the episodic plot the best for drama. In our view, however, the episodic plot of *Mother Courage* serves to reiterate its theme, war profiteering. Such a plot is also very effective for dramatists whose view of life emphasizes the diffuse nature of human existence, and whose dramas seek to address the broader powers that seem to operate on our destinies. After all, we may understand any particular "scene" in our day-to-day life, but don't we sometimes feel the "big picture" that unifies these episodes is past our understanding?

The main emphasis of our book is not, however, on these plot forms or their many variations. We are going to focus on drama built out of the structural parts mentioned at the beginning of the chapter. This type of plot has proven itself the gold standard of drama, and its parts, the most successful, battle-tested, sure-fire tools for delivering the kind of coherent story-experience that audiences the world over seem to crave.

At the same time, we feel constrained to point out to the writers reading this (and we sincerely hope that at least *some* of you are writers) that merely imposing this structure onto your drama will not, in and of itself, guarantee it will be good—or even successful. The quality of your story depends on your insight, your talent, and your uncompromising search for the truth. No study of the structure of any particular plot form can substitute for that. You could take every screenplay seminar in Hollywood and read every book ever written on playwriting, and still strike out, artistically and commercially. What such a study can do, however, is provide you with an understanding of the tools that dramatists have used over the centuries to shape their insights into compelling and exciting drama, and apply those lessons to your own work.

Finally, we want to reiterate a point we made earlier: we're going to examine these parts individually even though it will become apparent that they are all interdependently related. As we said, it is not a perfect solution, but it is a compromise we have to make. So, without any further ado, let's begin with …

The Leading Character

If you look up the word *protagonist* in the dictionary, you will find some of the following definitions: "first actor," "one in whom action centers," "one who takes the lead in any great matter," "advocate," "an active participant," "leader of an opposition," "a contender," and "one who takes the leading part in a drama, novel, or story; hence, an active participant or leader." The word actually derives from the ancient Greek, meaning the first (*pro*) speaker in a contest or debate (*agon*). We call this person the leading character.

The leading character is the central player in a struggle to achieve some goal. She is not simply someone with lots of lines or stage and screen time (although she may have both), but, more fundamentally, the character whose desires, actions, and fate in pursuit of her goal involve the viewer in the telling of the story. In short, the leading character is the person we look at and think, "This story is about her."

Not just any character can fulfill such a demanding role. The leading character shoulders the burden of the plot. For a couple of hours or so, an audience must be deeply interested in her life. From Dorothy to Macbeth, if the leading character is to succeed in engaging our attention and concern, several key requirements must be met.

First, and perhaps most obviously, she must actually appear *in* the story. An off-stage character, one talked about but not appearing, such as Sebastian Venable in Tennessee Williams's *Suddenly Last Summer* or Godot in *Waiting for Godot*, cannot be a leading character because it is through our viewing this character in *action* that the plot of a story is revealed.

Second, a leading character must be volitional, meaning she has the ability to make decisions and act upon them, rather than merely being acted upon. Decision-making includes choice, determination, and will power. A character who is incapable of choosing in any meaningful sense— a six-week-old baby or a person in a coma—will not make a good leading character because she cannot drive the story's arc of action. Can you think of any dramas that have such a leading character? Neither can we.

The leading character must also be thrown out of balance by an inciting incident, and, as a result, hit upon a conscious objective whose obtainment she hopes will restore equilibrium to her life. The inciting incident will be discussed in detail shortly, but characters who don't react to this event or seek any readjustment in response to it are too disinterested and passive to fulfill their function as the main character of the story.

Not only must the leading character have an objective, but she must also have the capability of pursuing it, as well as a chance of obtaining it. Although we may feel that the deck is stacked against Dorothy—how does a fourteen-year-old girl overcome a cyclone, a witch, and a wizard, not to mention that flock of flying monkeys?—we sense that Dorothy is smart and resourceful enough to succeed. Macbeth may be fighting long odds, but he is a renowned warrior and possesses an agile mind. Even though he ultimately fails to achieve his goal, we recognize that if anyone can pull it off, he can.

The leading character must also be able to put up an extended struggle to seek readjustment. If halfway through *The Wizard of Oz*, Dorothy simply throws up her hands, decides it's too dangerous and exhausting to get back to Kansas, and declares she would rather rent a small studio apartment in Munchkinland and play with Toto, she will not effectively function as a leading character. Neither will Macbeth if he tosses his broadsword on the ground once the going gets tough, and heads off for eighteen holes at St. Andrews followed by a plate of haggis. If these leading characters give up on their objectives, the audience gives up on them, which is only fair. If they aren't willing to stick it out 'til the end, why should we?

If, on the other hand, Dorothy is willing to march into the very heart of the Wicked Witch's lair and defeat her, go back and confront the terrifying and all-powerful Wizard and demand that he make good on his promise to return her to Kansas, *if* Macbeth is willing to defy not only his human adversaries but also battle the fates that have decreed his downfall, *if* he is willing to pursue his objective even after he learns of his wife's death and suspects his own, *then* we have the makings of leading characters willing to put up the kind of extended struggle necessary to keep us awake and in our seats.

But even all that is not enough to make us care. For that we need to empathize with the leading character. When we empathize with her, we imaginatively project ourselves into her consciousness and circumstances; we understand and relate to her needs, feelings, and behavior; we recognize ourselves in her, and we see her experiences and struggles as a reflection of our own. We move from "This story is about her" to "Hey, this story is about *me!*"

That we must empathize with the leading character does not mean that we must necessarily *sympathize* with her. When we empathize, we understand; when we sympathize, we support, encourage, or approve. Think of road rage. If someone violently cuts you off in traffic while yammering away on a cell phone and tossing litter out the window, we can empathize with your fantasy of running her off the road and into the back of a truck carrying a fully loaded port-a-potty that smashes through her windshield, covering her with its contents. But that doesn't mean that we want you to do it or will sympathize with you if you do. Well, *we* might, personally, but the police won't. In any event, a leading character must be empathetic, but she does not necessarily have to be sympathetic for us to empathize with her actions.

The *Wizard of Oz* and *Macbeth* offer a perfect example of this distinction. Dorothy is both empathetic *and* sympathetic. She's a young girl who wants to get back home after finding herself suddenly thrust into a dangerous situation. And she's looking out for her dog, Toto. Who can't relate to that? We want her to win.

Macbeth is another example. To be sure, we can empathize with his ambitions. It's human to crave influence and domination, even if we loathe admitting it. Furthermore, he fights against these excessive desires because he is basically a decent man, which further bonds him to us since we all know what it is to struggle with our conscience. Yet for all that empathy, we don't approve of his desires or actions. We don't want him to succeed. Our strongest response to Macbeth is not "Go for it!" but, as the great Shakespeare critic A. C. Bradley said, "What a waste!"[8]

There is one major exception to the empathy requirement. In comedy where the aim is to ridicule and satirize human foibles, such as greed, scorn, hypochondria, lust, gullibility, hypocrisy, or middle-class standards, we do not empathize with the leading character. For example, we are not asked to identify with, or feel for, the leading characters of Moliere's *The Miser*, *The Misanthrope*, or *Tartuffe*. They are too foolish or base to inspire an empathetic response. Why, then, do we sit through these dramas? Because we enjoy seeing such people brought down (if only we could do the same to their real-life counterparts!) and can't wait to see them get their comeuppance. Our empathy is reserved for the other characters in the story who are trying to make that happen.

Finally, the leading character is used to illustrate the author's point of view on the subject matter. In *Macbeth*, we see ruthless ambition leading to dehumanization and, ultimately, self-destruction; *Oedipus* shows us pride goeth before a fall; and Dorothy discovers that for all its problems, there's no place like home. It should be said that the reader may disagree that these are, in fact, the views illustrated by these leading characters. That's fine; the important thing to acknowledge is that the actions of the leading characters illuminate the authors' themes as interpreted by the directors and her artistic colleagues.

Up to this point we have been speaking of the leading character as a single character. That is usually the case. But on occasion, as in *Romeo and Juliet*, both title characters share the same inciting incident and the same objective—to be with one another—and the shifting fortunes of the story elate and desolate them equally. Sometimes there are three or more characters, as in the case of *The Flight of the Phoenix*, who merge into a collective leading character. When a plane crashes in the Saharan desert, all the survivors are thrown out of adjustment by this inciting incident and all pursue the same objective: to get out of the desert; if they do, they live, if they don't, they die.

In this group arrangement, it is not necessary that every character embody all the characteristics discussed above. One character might be less empathic than another; a third might be less willing to fight to the finish than a fourth. Nevertheless, when taken as whole, the group exhibits the same characteristics as a single leading character.

The other structural arrangement that involves more than one leading character is a story in which there are several different plots, each with a different leading character pursuing a different goal. Tony Kushner's *Angels in America* is an example. Joseph, Prior, Harper, and Louis each function as leading characters in their own plots. They are all responding to different inciting incidents and have separate objectives; what's good for one may not be good for, or even related to, another.

Films with multiple leading characters have become increasingly popular in recent years. Quentin Tarantino's *Pulp Fiction* has four separate stories, each with its own leading character. The same is true for Paul Haggis's *Crash*, dealing with racial intolerance in Los Angeles. One of the pleasures of such a structure is seeing how all the independent plots intersect and their characters interrelate.

To summarize the criteria for a leading character: (1) She is *in* the action that constitutes the story; (2) She is volitional; (3) She has the capability of achieving an objective, as well as a chance—however small—of actually succeeding, and she won't give up in that pursuit; (4) She *must* be empathetic; she *may* also be sympathetic; and (5) She serves to illustrate the author's point of view on the subject matter.

The Inciting Incident

"The other day," you start telling a friend, "I was walking down the street when, all of a sudden...." Or how about this: "I was on the subway, coming home from a party last night, and just as I was about to sit down...." Or surely you remember, "I was at the petting zoo last Tuesday, and when I bent over to feed the baby llama...." Whether you know it or not, in each of these examples, you are getting ready to describe the story's inciting incident.

In dramatic storytelling, either prior to the start of the story or soon after it begins, the leading character is thrown out of balance by a specific event. It is called the inciting incident because it forces the leading character into action to restore the balance that has been disrupted. This struggle to achieve readjustment determines the story's length: its beginning, middle, and end.

Prior to the inciting incident, we do not mean that the leading character is in a state of blissful harmony. For most of us, life is a decidedly pendular affair, swinging back and forth between boredom and excitement, pleasure and pain, failure and success. You find a dollar on the sidewalk, your cell phone battery dies in the middle of a call, you can't find your keys, a cute guy smiles at you on the bus; our lives are filled with these daily ups and downs that together create an existence we recognize as more or less normal.

The inciting incident of a story creates a far bigger disturbance in the leading character's life than these "thousand natural shocks that flesh is heir to." It is the signal event that, through its disruptive power, acts as the catalyst that sets the plot in motion. Once it occurs, the audience knows the story has begun in earnest.

In *Macbeth*, the inciting incident occurs in act 1, scene 3. Macbeth, coming from battle, encounters three witches on a desolate moor. At this point, his life is pretty much in a state of equilibrium. True, he has just emerged from life-or-death combat (in which he sliced his opponent in half), but this has not thrown his life unduly out of balance. He is a warrior in a warrior culture; slashing people with broadswords is a pretty normal activity.

For some time, however, he has been living with a murderous design to become king of Scotland. But hearing the witches' prophesy forecasting his eventual ascension to the throne causes an altogether riveting reaction in him. "Good sir, why do you start, and seem to fear things that do sound so fair?" Banquo asks, and just in case groundling Joe Six-Pack, standing in the yard of the Globe Theatre, has missed Macbeth's reaction, six lines later Banquo observes "he seems rapt withal," and 85 lines after that Shakespeare gives Macbeth a soliloquy to reiterate the moment.

This supernatural soliciting
Cannot be ill; cannot be good. If ill,
Why hath it given me earnest of success,
Commencing in a truth? I am Thane of Cawdor.
If good, why do I yield to that suggestion
Whose horrid image doth unfix my hair
And make my seated heart knock at my ribs
Against the use of nature?

Does this not look and sound like a man thrown out of adjustment?

The film version of *The Wizard of Oz*, though essentially a children's fable, has a more complicated structure: two separate plots that are interwoven into a single story, each with its own inciting incident.

The first plot concerns Dorothy's ongoing problems with Elmira Gulch, the severe and uncompromising landowner in the Depression-era farmlands of Kansas, where the story begins. Dorothy's dog Toto has a history of getting into Miss Gulch's garden and chasing after her cat, and Miss Gulch has a history of getting angry about it.

Then one day something different happens. Miss Gulch goes after Toto with a rake, Toto bites her, and she threatens to call the sheriff and have the dog put away. When Dorothy runs home and attempts to tell her aunt and uncle what happened, they admonish her to stop pestering them so they can attend to their chores. Going to Zeke to talk the situation over, she slips and falls into the pigpen. She even gives musical vent to her frustrations and hopes in "Over the Rainbow."

Yet, for all her problems, we are still left with the feeling that this is basically how her life operates. She will probably go on in this way into the foreseeable future had Miss Gulch not arrived, a letter from the sheriff in hand, demanding they turn Toto over to her so the "menace" can be snuffed out. Her aunt and uncle can't go against the law, so they hand Toto over to his tormentor.

To say this event throws Dorothy out of balance doesn't begin to describe its effect. She is devastated. But when Toto races home after leaping from the basket on Miss Gulch's bicycle, Dorothy decides on a plan to restore order and balance to her life: she and Toto will run away. Their belongings packed in a weathered suitcase, Dorothy and Toto hit the road, soon to encounter Professor Marvel, a traveling carnival performer. He understands she is a runaway and convinces her, by pretending to read his crystal ball, that her Aunt Em is suffering a broken heart over her disappearance. Panicked, Dorothy races home, and it is at this point that she comes face to face with the inciting incident of the second and main plot of the story: the twister that carries her away to Oz.

We call this the main plot because if you had one or two sentences to describe the film to someone who hadn't seen it, this is surely where you'd start. It's unlikely anyone would say *The Wizard of Oz* is about a young girl having her dog taken away by a mean neighbor. Most would accurately say that the film is about a girl from Kansas who one day finds herself lost in a strange world and who goes on a journey to return home. Only one event can truly be said to incite that main plot: the tornado.

The choice of where in the story's arc of action to place the inciting incident is extremely important. If the story is to interest and involve the audience—to hook them—the inciting incident must occur fairly early after the leading character is thrown out of adjustment.

On the other hand, if it comes too soon in the telling, the audience may not have a chance to develop an empathetic bond with the leading character, or understand the world she inhabits, and therefore may not be sufficiently invested in the story's outcome. For example, if *Hamlet* began with the title character wildly declaring his intention to avenge his father's murder, we would have no context in which to put his behavior.

Rather than identifying with him and his objective, we might think he was a nutcase.

That's why Shakespeare waits a few scenes, until we know more about the situation—Hamlet, his family, the "rotten" state of Denmark—before introducing the inciting incident. After Hamlet's conversation with his father's ghost and the revelation that his uncle murdered his father, Shakespeare's audience is ready to empathize with Hamlet's struggle to revenge his father's death.

Since there are no parenthetical stage directions written by the author, deciding where the inciting event occurs is a question of interpretation, and not all interpretations will be the same. In a brilliant Russian film of *Hamlet,* translator Boris Pasternak and screenwriter-director Grigori Kozintsev chose as the inciting incident the moment when Hamlet, studying in Germany, is informed of his father's death. This event occurs before the film begins. Indeed, under the credits we see Hamlet riding hell bent for leather along a rocky, surf-pounded Baltic shore toward a distant castle. Cut to the castle where colorful banners used to celebrate the wedding feast of Gertrude and Claudius are being replaced by black mourning flags draped through the parapets. Cut back to the rider. Clearly, in the film's first shots, this Hamlet is already out of balance and seeking some kind of readjustment.

Why, then, does the film succeed, given the above comments about needing time to identify with the leading character? We should understand that there is no written-in-stone rule governing the placement of the inciting incident. It is simply a matter of what works. The action—a man galloping on horseback—is inherently compelling. Our curiosity is aroused. "Why," we ask, "is that man racing toward the castle?" We're hooked! And once hooked we have time to receive the necessary information to engage our empathy for Hamlet and his objective.

Often the look of either the actors or their surroundings can induce an immediate empathetic response. Look at *The Wizard of Oz.* How much time do we really need before we fall in love with Judy Garland's Dorothy? One would have to have the heart of Ebenezer Scrooge not to melt just looking at her and Toto. And as for the world Dorothy lives in, identity is instantly established through the film's warm sepia-toned pictures of the desolate, Dust Bowl, Kansas landscape. By the time we hear Garland sing "Over the Rainbow"—less than six minutes into the movie—we are ready to follow her anywhere. In short, we're drawn in: hook, line, and sinker!

Another variation on the inciting incident is one in which the event happens but the leading character doesn't find out about it until later. An example of this occurs in the movie *Jaws*. Under the credits, the film opens with a beach party at night. A group of young people gathers around a fire. An attractive young woman catches the eye of a beer-drinking young man and indicates that she wants him to follow her. As she races down the dune, shedding her clothes for a skinny-dip, he attempts to keep up with her. Naked, she plunges in and swims out to deep water, but the young man passes out on the beach. In the stillness of the night, we suddenly hear the ominous beat of the theme music and the next thing we know, the woman has become a late night snack for a great white shark.

This happens three minutes into the story.

Cut to the home of the leading character, Chief of Police Brody, as he wakes up the next morning. A call informs him that a girl is missing. On the beach he questions the man who was with the woman the night before. Suddenly a deputy's whistle pierces the air. Embedded in the sand is a mutilated torso crawling with sand crabs. Visibly shaken, Brody removes his glasses and slowly turns to look out at the water.

The inciting event and the leading character have met up seven minutes into the story.

In the examples above, the inciting event occurs after the story begins. But sometimes it happens before the story begins. It is late at night at the beginning of Arthur Miller's *Death of a Salesman*. The leading character, Willy Loman, has met his son Biff that morning at Grand Central Station. They quarreled and it is this inciting incident that has thrown Willy out of balance and given him his objective: to find the source of his son's antagonism and to set their relationship right. The story's arc of action has already begun and is told to the audience via dialogue between Willy and his wife, Linda, in the first scene.

This process, of revealing necessary background information (back-story) to the audience through dialogue or narration, is referred to as *exposition*. When the inciting incident takes place off-stage or screen, to understand the story, exposition of one kind or another must be conveyed.

The last important function of the inciting incident is that it sets up what French nineteenth-century playwrights called the "obligatory scene." This comes at the end of the story when the leading character makes her last attempt to win her struggle with the forces opposing her. This scene is considered obligatory because, having started the story and having set up the main struggle between the leading character and who/whatever opposes her, the writer is obligated to deliver the showdown scene at the end or the audience will be disappointed.

Dorothy, swept away by the twister, has one overarching objective: to return home. She has no idea when she steps out through the door of her house into the Munchkin village that her journey will lead to a final con-frontation with the Wicked Witch or the Wizard of Oz. Neither does a first-time audience. But they intuit that by the end of the story, the dislocation the tornado caused will be resolved one way or another, and Dorothy will either make it home or not.

Macbeth's life could go in any number of directions after his first meeting with the witches. The murder of Duncan is not pre-ordained; nei-ther is Macbeth's final combat with Macduff. But whatever path the story takes, the audience expects some kind of final confrontation between Macbeth's "vaulting ambition" and the forces that rise up in opposition to it. If this scene does not materialize, the audience will feel cheated—some essential part of the drama is missing—and the meeting with the witches a mere gimmick to get the story started.

In summary, the inciting incident is the event that throws the leading character out of balance. It happens either before the story starts or shortly thereafter. Whenever it occurs, it forces her to choose an objective she believes will make her world whole again. The resulting journey defines the length of the drama, its beginning, middle, and end. It also sets up the "obligatory scene," in which the objective is either met or not. Exposition, in the form of background information and characterization, may be needed to sufficiently prepare the audience for the central conflict the inciting incident causes, as well as describing the incident itself if it takes place before the show starts.

Objectives

Imagine yourself crossing a busy intersection on foot. An inciting incident strikes: you slip on a banana peel in the middle of the street and feel yourself falling. As you fall, do you simply go limp and think, "Shoot! I slipped on a banana peel, again! Well, no point in resisting the force of gravity. I'll just have to wait until my body smashes onto the concrete."

Unlikely.

Whether it's flapping your arms, arching your back, twisting your torso, or screaming, no matter how futile or embarrassing the attempt may be, you immediately—and, in this case, unconsciously—try to restore the balance that was lost when you slipped.

That's how badly humans wish to live a life in balance, both figuratively and literally. And that is why in drama, when the leading character is thrown out of balance, she will always find an objective that she hopes will put her on her feet again. In the case of the banana peel escapade, this happens right away; in some situations, it may take the character a little time to figure it out. Either way, once the objective is decided upon, the struggle to achieve it forms the basis for the plot's central conflict.

Our lives are defined by our objectives. Life's constantly shifting circumstances, whether for good or bad, produce a steady stream of desires that need fulfilling. When we are hungry, we want food. When we are tired, we want sleep. When we are lonely, we want companionship. A human being with no such needs would, to draw on Sir Isaac Newton's laws of motion, remain at rest, doing nothing, for all eternity. Even our voices exist to meet our objectives. If we could get everything we wanted without using our voice, guess what? We'd never yell or speak.

People rarely analyze consciously what their objectives are at any given moment, or why they say what they say. When you're hungry, you don't wonder whether you need food. When you're tired, you don't sit down and ponder whether sleep would solve the problem. If you feel the urge to eliminate body waste, you do not—hopefully—analyze what to do. When you want to know the time, you ask, "What time is it?"

We have needs and we act on them—period!

But we are not imaginary characters, nor are our lives a selection of events arranged in a contrived sequence, as in a dramatized story. Everything we do—every impulse, every thought, every movement, every word—is filtered through the prism of our accumulated life experience. In dramatic storytelling, the characters have no such extended history that can be counted on to produce needs and desires. These backstories have to be created from the ground up, first by the author, then by the actors, directors, and designers. This process of creation necessitates conscious choices regarding objectives that real life rarely demands of us.

In dramatic storytelling, objectives broadly fall into two categories: *the through-line* objective the leading character has for the entire story, and the *beat, scene, and act* objectives throughout the story. Beat means the smallest unit of a character's intention with a beginning, middle, and end; several beats constitute a scene; and several scenes is an act. The through-line objective, decided upon when the leading character is thrown out of balance, never changes. She pursues that one goal, which she will obtain or fail to obtain by the story's end.

In each beat, scene, or act, however, she has smaller, less encompassing goals that feed into, contribute to, and further her through-line objective. It is the bond between these two objectives that makes for a coherent story. This process, creating conscious choices regarding objectives, is something that rarely exists in real life.

Let's talk about a real-life situation: Tom has an interview that could land him the job of assistant stage manager for the national touring company of a hit musical with a year's scheduled bookings. Obviously, he wants the job. His apartment is on Manhattan's Upper West Side. His through-line objective is "I need to get to the general manager's office at First Avenue and 43rd Street." His beat and scene objectives are: (1) I need to get to the subway; (2) I need to catch the express train; (3) I need to catch the shuttle over to Grand Central.

STANISLAVSKY ON BEATS

I left the Shustovs with my head full of ideas about units. As soon as my attention was drawn in this direction, I began to look for ways of carrying out this new idea.

As I bade them goodnight, I said to myself: one bit (pronounced "beat," by Mme Ouspenskaya in Boleslavsky's American Theatre). Going downstairs I was puzzled: should I count each step a unit? The Shustovs live on the third floor—sixty steps—sixty units. On that basis, every step along the sidewalk would have to be counted. I decided that the whole act of going downstairs was one, and walking home, another.

How about opening the street-door; should that be one unit or several? I decided in favor of several. Therefore I went downstairs—two units; I took hold of the door knob—three; I turned it—four; I opened the door—five; I crossed the threshold—six; I shut the door—seven; I released the knob—eight; I went home—nine.

I jostled someone—no, that was an accident, not a unit. I stopped in front of a bookshop. What about that? Should the reading of each individual title count, or should the general survey be lumped under one heading? I made up my mind to call it one. Which made a total of ten.

By the time I was home, undressed, and reaching for the soap to wash my hands I was counting two hundred and seven. I washed my hands—two hundred and eight; I laid down the soap—two hundred and nine; I rinsed the bowl—two hundred and ten. Finally I got into bed and pulled up the covers—two hundred and sixteen. But now what? My head was full of thoughts. Was each a unit? If you had to go through a five act tragedy, like Othello, on this basis, you would roll up a score of several thousand units. You would get all tangled up, so there must be some way of limiting them. But how?

Today I spoke to the Director about this. His answer was: A certain pilot was asked how he could ever remember, over a long stretch, all the minute details of a coast with its turns shallows and reefs. He replied: "I am not concerned with them; I stick to the channel."

So an actor must proceed, not by a multitude of details, but by those important units which, like signals, mark his channel and keep him in the right creative line. If you had to stage your departure from the Shustovs you would have to say to yourself: first of all, what am I doing? Your answer—going home—gives you the key to your main objective.

(continues)

STANISLAVSKY ON BEATS (*continued*)

Along the way, however, there were stops. You stood still at one point and did something else. Therefore looking in the shop window is an independent unit. Then as you proceeded you returned to the first unit.

Finally you reached your room and undressed. This was another bit. When you lay down and began to think you began still another unit. We have cut your total of units from over two hundred down to four. These mark your channel.

Together they create one large objective—going home.

Constantine Stanislavsky, *An Actor Prepares* (New York: Theatre Arts, 1936), 106–107.

At Grand Central, he goes up to the main concourse and, glancing at the clock atop the information booth, he sees that he has fifteen minutes to get to the office, which is six very long blocks away. His objectives then become: (1) I need to catch a taxi, (2) arrive at my destination, (3) interview, and (4) get the job.

Note in the text box how beats are reduced to manageable units; that is why, in the above example, there are only a few rather than two hundred.

It is very important that objectives be defined in specific, rather than general, terms. Dorothy's through-line objective in the realistic Kansas scene is, "I want to save Toto." Once she has been deposited by the cyclone in Oz it is, "I want to get back home." But these statements are too general to serve as the objectives for her choices and actions in each beat, scene, and act. Her *means* of getting back home is developed by objectives in the smaller units. Three of them are: "I wish to get to the Emerald City"; "I wish to have an audience with the Wizard"; and "I wish to persuade him to help me to get home;"—all specific enough for an actor to play and an audience to comprehend.

Although Macbeth is ambitious for power, ambition and power are abstract ideas, not objectives. His specific through-line objective is, "I wish to become King of Scotland." Two specific *means* to this end are: "I will murder King Duncan"; and "I will kill McDuff if he stands in my way." If the actor tries to lump together the beat, scene, and act objectives in such a statement as, "I will force into submission anyone who potentially stands in my way," he will find such a statement too general to act. The smaller units must be worded in such a way as to connote a specific *action*. By its very definition then, such an objective faced with an obstacle will result in *dramatic conflict* necessary to interest an audience.

The same is true even in a soliloquy such as Hamlet's "To be or not to be?" Hamlet is alone. His objective is to decide whether or not to commit suicide. But when we ask questions, we typically want answers—even if these answers come from ourselves. Is Hamlet simply deliberating the pros and cons of suicide throughout the soliloquy? Or, in the beats of this tough personal question, is he demanding answers, forcing, prodding, challenging *himself* to decide, "Should I suffer the wrongs Claudius has inflicted on me or just end my life?" The former might very well be intellectually stimulating; the latter—revealing conflict within himself—makes for dramatic storytelling that is capable of holding an audience.

Audience empathy is largely based on an understanding not only of what the character wants, but also of how badly she wants it and what she is willing to do to get it. Although Dorothy's through-line objective is to get home, it is in the smaller, more specific units of objective that constitute her means to this end and show that she is willing to brave fierce obstacles in order to see the Wizard, who she believes will help her. It is in these smaller units that Macbeth is willing to kill a king and see his wife slip into dementia in order to sate his ambition. Chief Brody is willing to risk his fear of the sea to pursue a man-eating shark. Romeo and Juliet are willing to risk banishment and even death to be together.

It's hard to find higher stakes than these.

In addition, the specific objective must also include urgency; that is, the leading character must pursue what she wants without delay. Dorothy sets out on the yellow brick road at almost the moment she is told it will take her to the Wizard. Macbeth is writing his wife of the encounter with the witches before he has even returned to the castle. Although it takes some prodding from her, the plan to murder Duncan is put into practice that very night. There's no waiting, no dallying, no relaxing for either of these two leading characters because their objective is vital and has to be fulfilled *now!*

Are characters as aware of their objectives as are the actors who seek to breathe life into them? Yes, because dramatic storytelling is reductive in that sense; but in everyday life, we rarely encounter people so single-minded and fixated on one simple through-line objective. In real life, we get distracted, multiple duties intrude—life happens—so what seems vitally important one day is pushed to the back burner till the next day and the day after that. But drama must distill down to its very essence the passions and needs that drive its characters, and it should clarify these impulses to give them meaning and allow audience insight. Leading characters must be relentlessly focused on achieving what they seek. Otherwise, there is no true volition.

However we think of a character's objectives, and *whatever* words we use to describe them, if they are to have practical value, they must run smack into the forces that block them. These forces are collectively referred to as ...

Obstacles

Merely having an objective does not a dramatic story make. If you were to write a one-act play or make a short film using the real-life stage manager story above, and you did not add obstacles, you would end up with a simple action that would make a story as dull as dishwater. What needs to be added? Empathy for the character and his through-line objective, high-stakes urgency, and, above all, obstacles that impede the character's objective, which will result in conflict-filled actions that make for sweaty armpits.

Picture young stage manager Tom, waking, tousled-haired, and looking anything but happy in his rattrap studio apartment on Manhattan's Upper West Side. Through the window, he sees blowing snow. He gets out of bed. Returning from the bathroom, shivering, he opens the door of his small refrigerator. It is empty except for two crusts of bread and an almost empty jar of peanut butter. He pops the bread into the toaster.

Finishing the last bite, the phone rings. It's Michael, an old school chum and production stage manager of the national company of the latest smash Broadway hit musical now playing in Los Angeles. Mike tells him the assistant stage manager has just quit. Mike has called the show's general manager in New York, who lives on East 43rd Street, and recommended Tom as a replacement. He's set up an interview for 11:00. Tom glances at the clock. It is 9:30. "What's the weather there?" Mike asks.

"It's snowing."

"In the low seventies here," Mike purrs. "Well, how about it. You interested?"

"You bet!"

Finishing combing his hair, Tom looks in the mirror. "I gotta get this job!" he tells his reflection. Running down the steps, he leaves the apartment, sees a cab coming down 8th Avenue, checks his wallet. He has exactly six bucks.

He races toward the subway entrance on Broadway. As he runs down the steps, he hears the train pulling in. There's a line at the turnstile. The lady just in front of him has a problem swiping her metro card, but she keeps trying. She gives up and, just as he swipes his own card, the train doors close. From the platform he watches as the Broadway #1 pulls away. He checks his watch. It is 10:10.

He arrives at 42nd and Broadway and decides to shuttle over to Grand Central. He races toward the stairs. A woman with three children and a baby carriage calls to him.

"Sir, can you please help me?"

He sees the baby asleep inside the carriage, "Sure," he says.

"They keep moving us from one hotel to another," she explains as they climb the steps.

Arriving at the top, she says, "God bless you."

"Good luck," he says and turns right toward the shuttle's platform. A swarm of people just off the uptown N and R trains are headed for the exit. The shuttle looks as if it is going to take off. He can't miss it! Pushing aside a meandering tourist, he just makes it as the doors begin to close.

He pulls hard to open them. The conductor finally releases the doors and he slips in.

At Grand Central, going up the escalator, a handholding out-of-town couple don't seem to realize they should stand in single file on the *right* side so those in a hurry can walk up on the left. "Excuse me," he says. The couple does not hear. "Excuse me!" he shouts.

Once in the main concourse, he encounters crowds of people. He checks the clock on top of the information booth. It's 10:42 and six long blocks away. To a stage manager, ten minutes ahead of the rehearsal call is *on* time. He decides to catch a taxi. But where from? Vanderbilt Avenue or in front of the terminal on 42nd Street? He decides on the front and races for the street. But the traffic goes west, and he has to cross the street to catch the cab. Just as he starts across, the light changes and traffic surges toward him.

He jumps back to the curb and waits for the light to change. As he starts to cross, he spots a cab that an Upper East Side matron, loaded down with packages, has hailed and is now moving toward. His need is greater than hers! He races her for the door.

Those who do not know the specifics of Manhattan's geography will at least sense the high-stakes urgency, along with the obstructions Tom runs into, that impede his objective. Haven't we all been in such a situation whether in New York City or Oshkosh?

The result of the interaction, or competition of needs, is bound to produce dynamic human conflict. And of course, it must be remembered that what we consider an obstacle to our goal is often what other people consider their objective. In Tom's story, nobody is walking around thinking, "I'm going to impede that guy's progress toward his destination, and, by doing so, stand in the way of what he is seeking to obtain." No. They're all too busy pursuing their own objectives and to them, Tom may be a problem! Even the most seemingly insignificant character in a film or play must have something they are pursuing.

Okay, you finish the story. Do you want Tom to make the interview and get the job? The ways in which obstacles present themselves and interact with the leading character are as limitless as the creativity of the artists involved. The struggle between objective and obstacle forms the heart of drama. It accounts for everything between the inciting incident and the story's climax. This battle is sometimes referred to as *progressive complications*. Progressive, because in most dramas, these obstacles progress in intensity and difficulty as the story unfolds; complications, because the obstacles complicate the leading character's attempts to reach her goals.

Equally important, progressive complications provide the audience with reference points for determining the shifting fortunes of leading characters as they struggle to achieve their objectives. Ideally, every beat, scene, and act of a drama should bring the leading character either closer or farther away from her goal. A beat represents a relatively small change of fortune, a scene is a more significant change, and an act represents a major shift. Indeed, the main function of beats, scenes, and acts is to mark these

TWO TYPES OF PLOTS: REVERSALS AND RECOGNITIONS

There are two types of plot: the *simple* and the *complex*.... By a "simple action" I mean one which is single and continuous ... whose change of fortune comes about without a reversal or recognition scene. By a "complex" action I mean one whose change of fortune is brought about by a reversal or a recognition scene, or both. These [reversals and recognitions] must grow out of the arrangement of the plot itself by its being so constructed that each succeeding incident happens necessarily or according to probability from what has happened previously; for it makes a great deal of difference whether the incidents happen because of what has preceded or merely after it.

A *reversal* is a change ... by which the action veers around in the opposite direction, and that, too, as we said, in accordance with the laws of probability or necessity.... As the name makes clear, *recognition* is a change by which those marked [by the plot] for good or for bad fortune pass from a state of ignorance into a state of knowledge which disposes them either to friendship or enmity towards each other. The best type of recognition is one which is accompanied by reversal.

Aristotle, *Poetics*, 20–21 (emphasis added).

plot movements. Aristotle called these movements "reversals,"[9] because they fundamentally redirect the trajectory of the leading character's journey toward her goal. Suspense is created in the audience as it wonders where the final shift in fortune will fall.

Just as objectives in drama tend to be more focused and urgent than in our everyday lives, so the obstacles facing the characters often tend to be more difficult and frustrating than those we are likely to encounter. Dramas tend to focus on these overwhelming obstacles for two reasons. First, they provide great conflict and suspense, and are therefore very exciting. Second, they also aid in creating audience empathy. If all Dorothy has to do to return to her Kansas farm is to say she wants to go home, her problem will not seem worthy of our attention. If Macbeth only has to ask for the crown to receive it, we will not engage ourselves in his quest. In short, a drama is only as compelling as the forces blocking the leading character's objectives make it.

One can identify obstacles in any number of ways, but broadly speaking they fall into two categories: internal and external.

Internal Obstacles

As the name suggests, internal obstacles are those that originate within the mind, heart, or body of the character.

For much of the early part of the tragedy, guilt is Macbeth's primary obstacle. He knows killing King Duncan is wrong and struggles with his conscience. At one point, it seems as though this obstacle might even overpower him. "We will proceed no further in this business," he tells his wife, before she shames him into action. Later, his guilt produces a hallucinatory dagger in the air, a "dagger of the mind," he calls it. After the murder, as he descends from the king's chambers holding the bloody dagger, he is stricken with pangs of conscience, and laments to his wife that he hears a voice cry, "sleep no more. Macbeth doth murder sleep!"

In the early Kansas scenes of *The Wizard of Oz*, Professor Marvel pretends to see Aunt Em in his crystal ball, and he intimates that she is dying of a broken heart. Dorothy feels guilty about running away and decides to return home.

Fear is another internal obstacle. Among the many reasons that stop Hamlet from suicide is fear of the unknown;"the dread of something after death— / The undiscover'd country, from whose bourn / No traveler returns, puzzles the will, / And makes us rather bear those ills we have / Than fly to others that we know not of?"

In the Oz sequence, Dorothy has to confront her fears: a young girl, in a strange land, encountering not only the Wicked Witch of the West, but also her minions in bizarre and sometimes frightening forms such as flying monkeys and forests where angry trees talk.

In *Jaws,* Chief Brody represents all of us in his primal fear of the unknown. After viewing the body parts of the drowned young woman, as he slowly turns and looks out over the sea, we feel the goose bumps rising. This primal fear is a protective instinct, hot-wired into us. It is the reason a dog may take several turns on a perfectly manicured lawn, thinking he is beating down the grass so that he is not vulnerable to attack before squatting to defecate. In *Jaws,* John Williams has incorporated this primal fear in the throbbing music, first in the underwater shot of the young woman swimming and later as a leitmotif throughout.

Inner obstacles can also be limitations of the body. For James Caan in the film *Misery,* his broken legs, the result of a car accident, prevent him from escaping from his tormentor. An obstacle to the wooing of Lady Anne by Richard III is the fact that he is a hunchback, "not shaped for sportive tricks, nor made to court an amorous looking glass." In Arthur Kopit's *Wings,* the leading character, Emily Stilson, is a former stunt pilot now in her seventies who suffers a massive stroke. Her struggle to communicate with her doctors and physical therapist forms the central conflict of the play.

External Obstacles

Among the most compelling external obstacles in a story are characters referred to as "antagonists."

Macbeth's obsession in the first half of the play is how to eliminate his friend and rival, Banquo, who suspects that Macbeth has "played most foully" for the crown. "There is none but he whose being I do fear," Macbeth soliloquizes, pondering Banquo's assassination. At the drama's climax, Macbeth meets his death at the hands of a fellow nobleman, Macduff.

For Dorothy, a state of antagonism exists between her and Miss Gulch from the very first shot. As we noted earlier, her aunt and uncle have little time for her problems. Even the farmhands, busy with their appointed chores, seem to be blocking her need to be heard. Her most famous antagonists, however, appear in Oz itself: the Witch, the Wizard, and the Lion. The Wicked Witch is such a compelling and memorable antagonist that we are hardly likely to realize she only appears in the two-hour film for a total of approximately twelve minutes!

A major obstacle to Chief Brody pursuing his objective in *Jaws* is in the guise of an easy-going good guy—in short, a born politician—Amity's mayor, who represents the monied interests of the community. He first refuses to believe there even is a shark, and once convinced, he doesn't want Brody doing anything about it for fear it will interrupt the 4th of July weekend, the town's most profitable day of the year. Once Brody has forced the mayor into signing the contract with Quint to get the shark, another obstacle enters the picture—Quint himself—who must be persuaded to allow Brody and Hooper to accompany him on the voyage. Dubious of their seamanship, he challenges, "Maybe I should go alone." Brody fires back, "It's my party, it's my charter." "Yeah, it's your charter, your party. It's my vessel!" The attempt to get the shark seems like it will fall apart before the boat has even left the dock.

But of course the major obstacle in *Jaws* is Great White, the villain. We use this moniker in the old melodramatic sense of the word—as a one-dimensional character with no redeeming features and no causality to arouse understanding for his badness. No attempt, such as a flashback, picturing him as a cuddly, misunderstood baby shark being raised by a single mom in the skuzzy part of the ocean, is made to anthropomorphize his nasty habit of munching on human beings.

The other-people-as-obstacles device is so successful that an entire segment of the entertainment industry has been built around it alone: the soap opera. That is because soaps are about one thing only: personal relationships. Part of the unreality—and the pleasure—of these shows is that the characters deal with nothing other than relationship problems. Fans would probably be deeply dissatisfied if any profound existential crisis intruded. Finding out who is sleeping with whom, and what the aggrieved party is going to do about it, suffices.

External obstacles also cover those forces that go beyond any particular individual antagonist: fate, magical forces, social conditions, nature, and so on.

Macbeth is in conflict with more than just his conscience and the other Scottish thanes. As with leading characters since Oedipus, he must deal with the forces of fate as represented by the witches, whose appearance is so otherworldly and so mysterious that it is beyond the grasp of human understanding. Banquo says that they seem "not like the inhabitants o' th' earth."

For Dorothy, too, almost every obstacle she encounters in Oz—the talking trees, the flying monkeys, the Witch's private guard, the doorman at Emerald city, the field of sleep-inducing poppies, the Wizard himself, and the Wicked Witch—are imbued with magical powers that must be overcome if she is to succeed.

The popularity of the courtroom drama, such as in the novel *To Kill a Mockingbird*, is due in large part to the immense power generated by one of the most enduring of external obstacles: the institutions of the state. The hero, Atticus Finch—an underdog rather than the judge or a powerful attorney—is attempting to defeat the strength inherent in the criminal justice system by defending an African American man who is innocent of the crime of which he is charged. In addition, Atticus must fight against a toxic social problem, the perversity of racism, which has infected the court along with the entire fabric of the world in which the story takes place. Although individuals may, in fact, represent these obstacles, what gives these antagonists their power is the backing of a broader societal authority that far transcends their own.

Forces of nature as obstacles are abundantly illustrated in James Agee and John Huston's film *The African Queen*. In case you are one of no more than two people in North America who has not seen this film, let us give a quick synopsis and, while doing so, a review of the various structural parts of the plot already discussed with an emphasis on the specific obstacles.

During World War I, a German raid on an African village (the inciting incident) where Rosie Sayer (the leading character, played by Katharine Hepburn) and her brother, the Rev. Samuel Sayer (Robert Morley), are missionaries, results in the latter's death. In reprisal, Miss Sayer decides that she will go down the river and sink a German ship (through-line objective). But first she must convince rumpot "Captain" Charlie Allnut (Humphrey Bogart)—for the moment a personal antagonist, later, a co-leading character—to not only transport her on his rusty steamboat, *The African Queen*, but also agree to help her destroy the ship.

Rosie (and, later, both of them) encounters multiple obstacles on the journey: fear caused by the Germans who fire on them from a fort high on the embankment; fear from the very real possibility of being hanged; guilt on Rosie's part for deep-sixing all of Allnut's booze; personal antagonism by Charlie, who at first is against the plan; fate in the form of the falling off of *African Queen*'s rudder, forcing the couple to improvise a bellows—no mean trick in the middle of the jungle—in order to weld it back on; and designing a homemade torpedo to sink the German ship, which results in the story's ending, not with a whimper but with a bang!

But perhaps their most formidable obstacles are encountered in nature. These include shooting the rapids ("I never realized any mere physical experience could be so stimulating!" Rosie cries); the drying up of the river, which diminishes to a trickle and prevents the boat from moving; and swarms of mosquitoes, roving crocodiles, and, unforgettably, the leeches that cover Charlie when he gets out to push the boat.

In summary, obstacles are those forces that stand between the leading character and her objective. As with all the structural parts of plot, they are as unique, varied, diversified, and endless as Darwin's species. Without them, there is no story, as nothing would stop the leading character from immediately restoring the balance in life that was interrupted by the inciting incident. There would also be no truth, because if life shows us anything, it's that for every desire we have, something—overwhelming, insignificant, or somewhere in-between—is standing in our way of getting it.

Crisis

You come to a door. It's locked. You desperately need to get into the room!

Do you slam your body against it? Do you knock? Do you get out your cell phone and call 911? If getting through the door is really important to you, you take a moment to consider alternatives, weighing one action against another in search of the best solution. What you don't do is act without thought.

You make a decision.

If a playwright knows her craft, the leading character will be making decisions about actions in pursuit of her through-line objective in every beat, scene, and act of the drama. Toward the end of the story, however, she will be forced into making *a final decision* of greater importance and difficulty than any others she has made or will make. This decision is the one the audience has been waiting for, since the character was thrown out of balance by the inciting incident. It is called the *crisis*, and it will test the leading character's commitment and resolve to a greater degree than any previous decision. If written and played properly, it is arguably the most exciting and suspenseful moment in the production.

One point, however, needs clarification. When we say "final" decision, we don't mean the leading character stops making choices altogether. She continues making them, but now they relate strictly to *ways and means* of accomplishing the crisis decision.

Suppose, for example our character is being pursued by a psychopathic stalker. Her objective? Survival. Near the end of the drama the stalker—who she has just found is a serial killer—has her cornered in her apartment. She has a choice: jump out the window in the hope of escaping, subdue him, or, if need be, kill him with the pistol she carries in her purse (the play takes place in Texas). All options carry great risks. If she jumps, it's four stories down; if she stays, the stalker—armed and more experienced in killing than she—would undoubtedly attempt to kill her. Neither option guarantees her survival. After an agonizing moment, she chooses to fight it out. This is her crisis decision. Yet she still has decisions to make. Should she greet him as though she is not afraid and infer that they could be friends? Should she have the gun cocked and ready to fire as he opens the door? Or would it be better if she hid the gun under her pillow and then pulled it out as he approached? If so, should it be cocked or should she do that just before firing? These are difficult choices, but none as difficult or as important as the crisis decision she has already made: irrevocably committing to killing her antagonist.

In the theater, the decision is often verbalized, but it may occur in silence, particularly in films, since it is possible for close-ups to project the character's inner thoughts and feelings—not to be confused with "indicating" via clichéd facial expressions, gestures, or body language—to the audience.

An example of a nonverbal crisis occurs in *Jaws*. Chief Brody (along with his boat-mates) has made numerous attempts—using fish nets and reels, harpoons attached to barrels, pistol and rifle fire at short range—to bring about the end of the great white. None of the choices has worked. The shark not only lives, but it has also turned the tables and is pursuing his pursuers. The engine is burned out; the radio destroyed. Hooper is missing from the shark cage and presumed dead. The boat is sinking, and Quint has been eaten by the shark. With very few options remaining, Brody is pondering his next move when the great white crashes through the window of the half-submerged cabin, lunging straight for him. Spotting the scuba tank of compressed air—the very cylinder he has earlier been told could explode if mishandled—Brody makes his decision: he will toss the tank into the shark's mouth and blow the shark up.

Note that the crisis decision cannot by itself guarantee success. Brody's plan could still fail for any number of reasons. And that's exactly as it should be. A crisis decision that doesn't risk failure would be letting the leading character off too easily, undercutting the very thing the audience paid for: edge-of-their-seat, white-knuckled suspense. We *hope* Brody's decision will pay off, but we also need to fear it won't.

Death of a Salesman offers a first-rate example of what must be risked to achieve an important goal. In the play, Willy's objective is: "I want to find out, and therefore remedy, what is wrong in my relationship with Biff so I can help him to be successful." The obstacles are Biff as antagonist, Willy's social-economic values, and, most importantly, Willy's inability—based on Freud's theory that it is extremely difficult to face what is most painful to us—to admit that their relationship was shattered years ago when, as a senior in high school, Biff caught Willy in a hotel room with the woman from Boston.

In the crisis scene—the showdown between Biff and Willy—Biff says, "All right, phony! Then let's lay it on the line," and the two men fight. After "Biff's fury has spent itself, he breaks down, sobbing, holding on to Willy ... crying brokenly: 'will you take that phony dream and burn it before something happens?'" Struggling to contain himself, he adds, "I'll go in the morning" and exits.

> WILLY: (After a long pause, astonished, elevated) Isn't that remarkable? Biff—he likes me!
>
> LINDA: He loves you, Willy!
>
> HAPPY: (Deeply moved) Always did, Pop.
>
> WILLY: Oh, Biff! (staring wildly) He cried! Cried to me. (He is choking with his love, and now cries out his promise) That boy—that boy is going to be magnificent! (Ben appears in the light just outside the kitchen)
>
> BEN: Yes, outstanding, with twenty thousand behind him.

During the scene, the outcome is in abeyance. It is only when Willy "is choking with his love" just prior to "crying out his promise" that he is finally able to rip open his brain [the original title of the play was *The Inside of His Head*] and face his complicity as the cause of Biff's failure. With his brother Ben—the personification of The American Dream of success: ("When I was seventeen I walked into the jungle, and when I was twenty-one I walked out. And by God I was rich!")—taking shape in his mind, and understanding success only in terms of money, he makes his crisis decision. He will kill himself, leaving Biff his $20,000 life insurance policy; the only way he can show his love for his son and remedy the wrong he has caused. True, he has already thought of suicide (the rubber hose attachment to the gas pipe), but that incident happens outside the play's arc of action. Also true, within the play's arc, Willy borrows money from Charley to pay the premium on his insurance policy, but suicide is not a *fait accompli* at that point, and the audience hopes he will not resort to this means of accomplishing his through-line objective.

Note that the crisis often places the leading character in a position in which she must select between the lesser of bad options or equally good, but mutually exclusive, ones. Anything else lets her off way too easily. After all, if you were offered the choice between chocolate cake and a moldy orange, who would choose the orange? If you were forced to choose between a moldy orange and a rotten egg, that would be a tougher decision. They're both pretty awful choices. Or if you really wanted both a piece of chocolate cake *and* a crème brûlée, but only had enough money for one, that, too, would be tough. They're both great, but you simply can't have them both. And it is the tough choices we want the leading characters to make after investing our heart, soul, and time in their journeys.

In the film *When Harry Met Sally*, Harry's crisis decision comes down to whether he wants to remain in the comfort of his bachelor life or throw himself into a relationship with Sally, with whom he is in love. Both of these choices have big upsides. Harry has become accustomed to the life he has set up for himself, and change is hard. But he also feels a new and very powerful feeling for Sally and wants to be with her. The problem is, these desires are irreconcilable. They both have their attractions, but he must surrender one to get the other. He ultimately chooses Sally over his old life.

Yet another variation is when the crisis decision takes place out of the audience's sight. In the *Wizard of Oz*, the setup for the decision happens on-screen, but the actual choice takes place off-screen. Dorothy and her three companions, having braved many obstacles, are finally given an audience with the Wizard. This is the crisis scene. Expecting to receive his help, they are shocked to discover he will only aid them if they perform a near suicidal task: bring him back the broomstick of the Wicked Witch of the West.

This puts Dorothy into a terrible dilemma: She can refuse to accede to the Wizard's demand, which would mean foregoing his help and not ever getting home. Or she can agree to it, which, as the Cowardly Lion is quick to point out, could very likely end up with them dying. Dorothy faces a situation in which no choice is a happy one, yet choose she must. But before she can, the Wizard bellows at the Cowardly Lion, and, true to his name, he tears out of the Wizard's chamber, runs down the hall, and throws himself headfirst through a huge glass window.

The director and the writers made an important decision: To let the crisis moment be preempted by a comic scene. It would have been very difficult to have so important an event come either directly before or directly after so silly a moment as the Lion leaping through a window. Those involved decided to put the crisis decision off-screen, after the fade-to-black.

When the lights come up, Dorothy and her pals are walking through the forest on their way to the Witch's castle, with all the traditional accoutrements of witch hunting: a pistol, a large wrench, a butterfly net, and a spray can of "Witch Remover." These props, rather than any visible thought process, tell us that between the end of the last scene and the beginning of this one, Dorothy has made her crisis decision. She will go to the castle of the Wicked Witch and somehow, despite the enormity of the odds, attempt to return with the Witch's broomstick as the Wizard demanded.

Most crisis decisions are acted upon fairly quickly. Macbeth's decision—to fight Macduff—leads immediately to the climactic showdown between the two. Yet sometimes there is a delay between the crisis decision and the story's climax. Although the line was recently changed, in the original 1963 version of Edward Albee's *Who's Afraid of Virginia Woolf?*,[10] the leading character, George, makes his final decision just thirteen lines prior to the end of act 2 but does not act on it until close to the end of the play. He eventually asks a Western Union boy to deliver a telegram to his wife, Martha, with the message that their son is dead, which will destroy her. The delay between when George makes his decision and when he actually springs it on Martha in the third act allows time for tension to build, as the audience, having been let in on George's plan, anticipates the final showdown with his wife. The verbalization of this decision is brilliantly accomplished in fifty-five words, including seventeen ellipses, making it clear to the actor playing George that this is a spontaneous act, which strengthens the "illusion of the first time," making the audience believe that real things are happening to real people.

There are few moments more dramatic than when a leading character is thinking the situation through prior to making the crisis decision. This can happen in an instant, as in the case of Chief Brody, or over a more extended period of time, as with George. One of the biggest mistakes in production is to truncate or skip over this moment of decision, or worse, to negate it fearing that the time it takes to make the decision, if played honestly, will result in audience restlessness. Quite the contrary! If time is not taken by the actor to create the illusion of spontaneity, making the moment believable, the audience will feel the outcome of the story is predetermined and predictable. And predictability is the cardinal sin in performance.

THE ILLUSION OF THE FIRST TIME IN ACTING

This expression, first coined by American actor and playwright William Gillette, and taken up by succeeding generations of acting teachers, means just what it says: the actor must strive to create the illusion that her thoughts, actions, and responses are not rehearsed and premeditated but are spontaneously occurring, just as they do in real life. But as Gillette acknowledged, and as actors quickly discover in their first scene study class, it is difficult for them to memorize lines and movements in order to convince audiences that they haven't. It should be noted that Gillette's injunction only applies to those styles of acting in which a realistic illusion of real life is the aim. In presentational drama, such as ancient Greek tragedy or Japanese Kabuki, more value may be placed on formalistic conventions of speech and behavior than on creating the naturalistic expressions practitioners such as Gillette were seeking to reproduce.

Toby Cole and Helen Krich Chinoy, eds., *Actors on Acting: The Theories, Techniques and Practices of the World's Great Actors, Told in Their Own Words* (New York: Crown Publishers, Inc., 1970), 563–567.

The fact that the outcome is predetermined by the text has nothing to do with audience response. Having paid their money, audiences want to believe that Hamlet may *not* be killed, that Oedipus will *not* find out the truth, or that Chief Brody will *not* lose his battle against the shark. No matter how often they have seen a film or play, the audiences wants to believe that real things are happening to real people *at that moment.*

To summarize: The crisis scene—sometimes called "the showdown"—is the most forceful attack instituted by the obstacles to impede the leading character from reaching her objective. At the end of this scene, the leading character makes the crisis decision—an ultimate action she hopes will result in achieving her objective. It is typically the most significant risk-taking decision she will make in the course of the story, and it leads, immediately or after a passage of time, to the climactic showdown with the obstacles. The crisis decision is sometimes verbalized, sometimes made clear through the actor's thinking, or sometimes a combination of thought and physical action.

However it is conveyed, the crisis decision forces the leading character into choosing between the lesser of bad options or between mutually exclusive good ones. On occasion, the decision takes place offstage or screen, but because of the inherent drama of the crisis decision scene, it is most often witnessed by the audience.

Climax

The climax depicts the leading character's greatest struggle in the story's arc of action to effect a reversal of fortune, resolving for good or ill the central conflict triggered by the inciting incident.

The climax of *Jaws* starts just after Brody's decision to toss the tank in Great White's mouth. Instead of blowing him up, the tank lodges in the shark's black gums, and he slips out of the sinking cabin. Brody climbs out of the cabin window, and seeing the shark headed back to make what appears to be a final assault on the crippled vessel, which is now rapidly sinking, he sees the rifle rack and knows what must be done. Slinging the rifle's strap over his arm, he shinnies out on the boat's tilting mast. Perched precariously over the sea, he aims the rifle at the scuba tank, now barely visible in the shark's mouth, a couple of hundred feet in the distance.

Sure, you can assume that Brody, having served in the NYC Police Force, is a marksman, but you'd think twice before betting the farm (or even the back forty) that he'll hit the tank. It's this sense of doubt that keeps you on the edge of your seat, eyes riveted on the screen when he fires the first of six .30 caliber bullets. With one shot remaining, and Great White closing in, Brody mutters, "Show me the tank! C'mon, show me the tank! Blow up!" Then he fires. The bullet hits home, hurling the shark into a blood-red geyser of water, and Brody gives a triumphant whoop of victory. And celebrate he should, for it is at this point that the final reversal of fortune occurs. Brody has made good on the objective he has had ever since the shark appeared: to protect the town from danger. Except for tying up a few loose ends, the story is now effectively over.

Just after Macbeth's "To-morrow, and to-morrow, and to-morrow" speech, which seems to indicate he has given up, a messenger enters and tells him that the forest, Birnam Wood, has begun to move—in reality, soldiers are camouflaged with tree foliage—toward the castle. Macbeth makes his final decision to continue the fight, and the climax scene begins: "Ring the alarum bell. Blow wind, come wrack; / At least we'll die with harness on our back!" The battle rages on- and offstage until MacDuff meets Macbeth face to face, commanding, "Turn, hell-hound, turn." The two spar and hurl insults at each other: "Lay on, Macduff; And damn'd be him that first cries 'Hold, enough!'" The combatants exit fighting, and some moments later Macduff reenters with Macbeth's head.

In *Oedipus Rex*, the climax takes place offstage. The Greeks did not portray scenes of violence onstage. But what happened offstage is *reported* by a messenger who describes Oedipus's mother hanging herself and Oedipus gouging out his eyes. The reporting of these tragic events is done in such an immediate manner that the words spark the spectators' imagination, and they see the offstage action in their mind's eye, which may be more effective than actually seeing what happened take place in front of them.

In *Hamlet*, when Horatio advises Hamlet not to fence with Laertes, he replies: "Not a whit, we defy augury: there is a special providence in the fall of a sparrow. If it be now, 'tis not to come; if it be not to come, it will be now; if it be not now, yet it will come—the readiness is all. Since no man owes of aught he leaves, what is't to leave betimes? Let be."

Recognize that? That's right: Hamlet's crisis decision!

Having made his decision to fight, the play's climax begins with the sound of trumpets and drums and the entrance of the King, Queen, Laertes, and members of the court. At the end of this scene, dead bodies will strew the stage. Hamlet's mother will unknowingly drink poisoned wine and be in the first throes of death. Laertes will wound Hamlet with a rapier ("a hit, a very palpable hit"), the tip of which has been "envenom'd" (poisoned). In the "scuffle" that follows, the combatants' rapiers will be accidentally exchanged, and Hamlet will wound Laertes. The dying Laertes will then confess that the rapier was poisoned and that "Thy mother's poison'd …the King, the King's to blame." Knowing that there is very little time left before his own death, Hamlet will say, "the point envenom'd too! then, venom, to thy work," and stab Claudius.

In Ibsen's *A Doll's House*, Nora's husband Torvold, having opened the letter returning the promissory note which Nora signed, and knowing that she cannot now be incriminated for forgery, becomes solicitous in direct proportion to the anger he showed when he first found out about her deception. Now, as if seeing him for the first time, Nora makes her crisis decision. She goes offstage where she changes from her "fancy dress" to an everyday one. When she returns, she says, "Sit down, Torvold. You and I have a lot to talk about."

What follows—a roughly ten-minute confrontation in which she confronts her husband with her decision to leave—is the story's climax. With an understanding of the period's given circumstances, when husbands had almost complete control of their wives, her departure is in doubt. Torvold can force her to stay. Their confrontation ends, however, with Nora leaving the room, and we hear the outer door slam. She has freed herself from an oppressive relationship and set out on the journey to self-discovery that she views as her duty.

Notice how, in the above examples, once all the other parts of plot are in place, the climax may be described very briefly and with a minimum of analysis. If the leading character is strongly depicted, the inciting incident clearly established, the objective, obstacles, and crisis drawn sharply, the climax will seem surprising yet inevitable. We feel a satisfying sense of completion. "Of course," we tell ourselves, "the story had to end that way," even though we may not have anticipated how the struggle was going to be played out.

To summarize: The climax is the final and usually most intense showdown with all the forces of antagonism that have impeded the leading character's journey to achieve her objective. It is the highest point of conflict in the story's arc of action, as well as the final, and most affecting, reversal of fortune the leading character undergoes.

Resolution

We are eschewing the French word *denouement* (deh-noo-MAHN), meaning "to untie" the threads of the plot, not for the same reasons the U.S. Congress did away with French fries in its cafeteria when France refused to allow our planes to fly over their air space, but simply because the word "resolution" seems less formidable, although just as appropriate.

We define resolution as that part of the dramatic story that occurs after the climax and continues to the story's end. It includes the disentangling of the threads of the plot brought about by the central—as well as ancillary—conflicts. If the leading character achieves her objective in the climactic scene, she either returns to adjustment or, if she has failed to do so, there is a readjustment to the outcome, and a new equilibrium established.

One of the key functions of the resolution is to show the effects of the climax on the characters and their world. For many, a significant change has occurred and the audience—wanting to return to a world in which there is order rather than chaos—needs time to solidify the nature of that change. For example, after Macbeth has lost his battle with Macduff, we learn that Malcolm, King Duncan's son and the legitimate heir to the

Scottish throne, is to be crowned king. There is closure to the disruption caused by the inciting incident. A new balance has been achieved.

The same is true for *Hamlet*. After Hamlet's death, Horatio says: "Now cracks a noble heart. Good night, sweet prince, / And flights of angels sing thee to thy rest! / (*March within.*) / Why does the drum come hither? (*Enter Fortinbras and the English Ambassador, with drum, colours, and Attendants*)." The Ambassador says that Hamlet's commandment was fulfilled: "Rosencrantz and Guildenstern are dead." Horatio replies that "He never gave commandment for their death," and once that loose thread of the plot is tied, he goes on to suggest that "these bodies / High on a stage be placed in view." Horatio tells Fortinbras, who will become the new king, how the tragedy came about. Shakespeare then gives his audience a preview of the future by revealing the new king's character, and something of the new order that will follow. In his first command, Fortinbras specifies the arrangement of the burial which will honor Prince Hamlet.

Jaws ends with the pieces of Great White sinking in the ocean. Hooper, freed from the shark cage, surfaces and finds out that the shark is destroyed. The scene cuts to Brody and Hooper paddling toward shore on a piece of the boat attached to two of the flotation barrels. We can conclude that Brody's fear of the water has diminished, and that in the future Amity will continue to thrive as a seaside resort town with a safe beach. Brody and his family will flourish in this small town.

In Ibsen's *A Doll's House*, when Nora says goodbye to her husband and goes out through the hall, the climax is complete. The resolution consists of the following:

> HELMER: (Sinks down on a chair by the door and buries his face in his hands.) Nora! Nora! (Looks around and gets up.) Empty! She's gone! (A hope strikes him.) The Miracle of miracles? (The street door is slammed shut down stairs.)
>
> End of play

We can't know for certain the lasting effects the climax will have on the leading character, but we feel fairly confident there is a very good chance Nora will triumph in her search for self-identity. Conversely, we see Helmer as a broken man—a man conditioned to yield to society's conventions rather than living as an individual true to himself. Some viewers will hope that "the miracle of miracles" will occur, and he will change and perhaps the couple will be reunited. But the sound of the slamming door would seem to indicate that the social mores that have been bequeathed to and instilled in Helmer will preempt much hope for such a conclusion.

Resolutions don't necessarily need to be long. In *Dial M for Murder*, it is the leading character, Tony, who makes the readjustment and does so without uttering a single word. At the end of the climactic scene in which he is irretrievably trapped, actor Maurice Evans, creating the role in its New York premiere, provided the play's resolution by merely dropping his shoulders. Through the simple relaxing of body tension, we saw he had given up and was adjusting to the inevitable: he would either go to prison for life or be hanged.

The resolution not only brings closure to the main plot's entanglements but must also do the same for subplots that are related to the main plot but of lesser importance. In Shakespeare's *The Merchant of Venice*, for example, the climax scene is now considered to be when Portia—disguised as a lawyer—triumphs over Shylock in the courtroom scene.

Even after Shylock's defeat, however, the play's romantic subplots still need to be resolved. *The Merchant of Venice* is a comedy and, at the time it was written, that meant the lovers had to wind up happily together. Although the highest point of conflict in the story's arc of action has already occurred, closure of the romantic subplot must take place. In addition, there is the matter of the rings, which Portia and Nerissa gave their husbands who vowed never to part with them, but they did so, giving them to the "lawyer" (Portia in disguise) and "his assistant" (Nerissa in disguise) who helped win Antonio's freedom.

And perhaps most interesting of all, there is the matter of the older, enigmatic Antonio, who agreed to give a pound of his flesh to the moneylender Shylock as collateral for his dearest young friend Bassanio's loan, and whose ships, since waylaid, allow Shylock to demand the forfeiture of his payment. Antonio is saved by Portia, now Bassanio's wife, and as the young couples Grazino and Nerissa, Lorenzo and Jessica, and, more to the point, Portia and Bassanio exit giggling into the palace to consummate their marriages, Antonio is left onstage; the only possible resolution for *his* arc of action is that it must remain unresolved.

Audiences are drawn to dramatic storytelling to find a sense of closure rarely achieved in real life, where one or a series of events seem to lead seamlessly into the next. In most drama, such closure takes a bit of time. If a story ends too abruptly, particularly if the climactic reversal of fortune has been a tragic or upsetting one, the audience will be deprived of the necessary time to collect its thoughts and emotions. If, in the very moment Hamlet finished uttering his famous last words, "The rest is silence," the curtain fell, many in the audience would feel cheated of an important sense of completion given in the play's resolution.

The *Deus ex Machina*

Some resolutions have what is called a *deus ex machina*. This is Latin for "God from a machine" and refers to the Greek practice of using ropes and

---

DEUS EX MACHINA

It is also necessary in character portrayal, just as it was in arranging the incidents, to aim always at what is necessary and what is probable in such a way that when a certain type of person says or does a certain type of thing he does so either from necessity or probability; and when one thing follows another, it shall do so either from necessity or probability. It is evident, therefore, that the dénouement of a plot must result naturally from the plot itself and not from a *deus ex machina* as in the *Medea*, nor as it happens in the return of the *Iliad*. The *deus ex machina* must be used for matters outside the drama, for antecedent elements which it is not possible for man to know, or for subsequent matters which need to be reported or foretold; for we attribute to the gods the ability to see all things.

Aristotle, *Poetics*, 30.

pulleys to lower a character representing a god onto the stage at the play's end to resolve all the plot complications. It has come to mean the use of any improbable or random occurrences that function in this way.

Medea, by Euripides, offers a classic example of such a device. Medea and Jason have two sons and live happily together in Corinth until Jason leaves Medea for Creusa, the daughter of King Creon. In revenge, Medea sends a robe to the bride as a wedding present, which when donned ignites, cremating her. Then, in a final act of revenge, Medea kills the children.

Medea has achieved her objective, but what is to happen to her after the crimes she has committed? Since there is no probable way for her to escape Jason's wrath, Euripides has Apollo send her a golden chariot, pulled by dragons, no less, to carry her off. Voilà!

As is evident in the previous text box, both in ancient and modern times, the use of the *deus ex machina* device in solving a story's resolution—rather than having the leading character do so—has often been considered a weakness in plot structuring since it sidesteps *probability*. It negates what Samuel Coleridge saw as "that willing suspension of disbelief for the moment, which constitutes poetic faith."[11]

But how is *The Wizard of Oz* resolved? At its climax, Dorothy is on the brink of achieving her objective of returning to Kansas. At the gala send-off, with the Wizard at the helm, his hot-air balloon becomes untethered and floats off. "Come back, come back," Dorothy pleads. "Don't go without me! Please come back!" "I can't come back," the befuddled Wizard shouts, "I don't know how it works!" In despair, Dorothy wonders how she will ever get home. Suddenly the Scarecrow points upward. "Look," he calls, "here's someone who can help you!" Out of the sky, Good Witch Glinda descends in her pink bubble. Dorothy asks if she will help her. "You don't need to be helped any longer," Glinda purrs sweetly. "You've always had the power to go back to Kansas. . . . [You] had to learn it for yourself."

The Tinman asks Dorothy what it is she has learned. She answers: "If I ever go looking for my heart's desire again, I won't look any further than my own backyard. Because if it isn't there, I never really lost it to begin with." Smiling with approval, Glinda repeats, "There's no place like home," and Dorothy, intoning this mantra while clicking her ruby slippers, is transported back to Kansas and the tender ministrations of her beloved Auntie Em and Uncle Henry.

Then why, we might ask, since *deus ex machina* resolutions reduce the power of the leading characters in deciding their fate, have authors occasionally turned to this device? Aristotle acknowledges that in *a few* dramas, human action *can be* insignificant, compared to the workings of the gods.[12] An example is the classic 1953 science-fiction film, *The War of The Worlds*. The enemy was slain, after all of man's defenses failed, "by the lowliest living microorganisms that God in His wisdom put upon earth." A drama that has this point of view of life—that God is wise and humans are powerless—*must* turn to a *deus ex machina* for its resolution; any other would be false.

Generally, the reason people find the *deus ex machina* troubling is that they understand instinctively that it is a false resolution, because in real life their problems are not resolved by the miraculous intervention of a god or a random event. The reason some writers resort to this kind of resolution is not to fulfill some religious world-view, but more often for a lack of insight, craftsmanship, and creativity that holds the mirror up to life.

To summarize: The resolution is everything that occurs from the finishing of the climax to the curtain. It serves three basic functions: to show the effects of the climax on the characters and their world, to allow time to untangle the threads of any subplots that have not come to a conclusion, and to allow the audience time to reflect and assess the story's events before leaving the theater.

Summary of the Seven Structural Parts of a Plot

In Shakespeare's *Romeo and Juliet,* the leading characters are named in the play's title. The inciting incident is their meeting at a dance and falling in love. Their objective is to be allowed to be together and fulfill their love. The major obstacles are their feuding families, the Capulets and the

Montagues, and fate ("A pair of starcrossed lovers"). Romeo's crisis decision occurs in Mantua, when Balthasar enters and tells him that Juliet is buried in the Capulets' monument. "Is it e'en so?" Romeo replies. "Then I defy you Stars." "I do beseech you sir, have patience," Balthasar says, "Your looks are pale and wild, and do import some misadventure."

The reason Romeo's looks are pale and wild is that the message from the Friar, telling him of the plan to put Juliet into a sleep that will be mistaken for death, never reached him, and thinking she is dead, he makes the decision to kill himself to be with her. The actor playing the role would make this decision just before "Then I defy you Stars" and then clarify his words by saying, "Well, Juliet, I will lie with thee tonight."

His decision leads to the climax scene: his arrival at the Capulets' monument, the fight with Paris and his speech to the "dead" Juliet. It ends with his drinking the poison: "Oh, true apothecary / Thy drugs are quick. Thus with a kiss, I die."

Juliet's crisis decision occurs after she wakes and Friar Laurence, who has come to the tomb, informs her that "A greater power than we can contradict / Hath thwarted our intents. Come, come away; / Thy husband in thy bosom there lies dead." It is at this moment that she makes her decision to join Romeo in death. This moment of decision is the reason the Friar says, "Stay not to question for the watch is coming. / Come, go, good Juliet. I dare no longer stay."

> JULIET: Go, get thee hence, for I will not away.
>
> (Exit Friar Lawrence.)
>
> What's here? A cup, clos'd in my true love's hand?
>
> Poison, I see, hath been his timeless end.
>
> O churl! drunk all, and left no friendly drop
>
> To help me after? I will kiss thy lips;
>
> Happly some poison yet doth hang on them,
>
> To make me die, with a restorative.
>
> Thy lips are warm.
>
> (WATCH within) Lead boy. Which way?

The Climax.

JULIET: Yea, noise? Then I'll be brief. Oh happy dagger!

This is thy sheath; there rust and let me die.

(She stabs herself and falls on Romeo's body.)

If played uncut, which it almost never is, the play's resolution—an incredible 140 lines—gives information, most of which, we have just witnessed. This resolution is not only the bane of directors but was considered an "aesthetic blunder" by critics Johnson and Malone.[13] But Verona's prince, ignorant of what happened, must be informed before he can take any action. The bodies of Paris and Romeo and Juliet must be discovered by the watch; Prince Escalus, the Capulets, and the Montagues, must be summoned; and Friar Laurence must be brought back to explain to the prince what happened.

This plot reiteration starts with the Friar's unfortunate line, "I will be brief," and goes on for forty lines. Romeo's man must then testify and give Escalus Romeo's last letter to his father; the Prince must admonish the Capulets and Montagues for their hate and the resulting deaths of the children; the feuding families must be reunited in sorrow, friendship, and love after hating one another for years; and the Montagues must cement their future relationship by pledging to raise a statue in pure gold to the young lovers.

Puh-*leeze*, get the hook!

Staging a play is largely an exercise in problem solving. We offer a possible solution. The first to enter after Prince Escalus are the Capulets and, within a few lines, Capulet says, "Oh, heavens! O wife, look how our daughter bleeds!" Then Montague (and clan) enter telling the prince that his wife died during the night from grief of Romeo's exile. The prince then says,

Seal up the mouth of outrage for a while,
Till we can cure these ambiguities,
And know their spring, their head, their true descent;
And then will I be general of your woes,
And lead you even to death. Meantime forebear,

And let mischance be slave to patience.
Bring forth the parties of suspicion.

At which time the Friar appears and, within five lines, utters his famous "I will be brief" speech, which goes on for some forty lines. As he starts this speech to the prince, it becomes inaudible (perhaps only sometimes) to a pantomime revealing Juliet's mother breaking down and her husband comforting her. Montague breaks down over his son's body, and the families slowly unite in their grief, even embracing and comforting one another in sorrow—a handclasp by the fathers and whispering pledges to raise a statue as a memorial to their children.

By this time, the Friar, Balthasar, and the Page are finished, and the prince addresses the families: "Capulet, Montague, see what a scourge is laid upon your hate." Then Capulet says, "Oh, brother Montague, give me thy hand," etc., and we will have shown, *through action*, the families coming together.

* * *

This chapter is the longest in the book. This is not an accident. When we tell a story or describe a play or film to a friend, we start with the plot. Other elements of dramatic architecture, however important, will most likely go for naught if the plot of the story fails to engage the audience.

We will return to these plot elements at various points in the book to demonstrate the interdependency of all the component parts of dramatic architecture. For now, it is enough to refer back, as we often do, to Aristotle. Plot, he said, is the very "soul" of drama.

Notes

1. To download a copy of *The Wizard of Oz* screenplay, visit http://www.un-official.com/The_Daily_Script/ms_wizoz.htm.

2. Eugene Ionesco, *Four Plays*, trans. Donald M. Allen (New York: Grove Press, Inc., 1958), 42.

3. August Strindberg, *A Dream Play and Four Chamber Plays*, trans. and intro. Walter Johnson (New York and London: W. W. Norton & Company, 1975), 19.

4. Harold Taylor, *Art and Intellect* (New York: The National Committee on Art Education for the Museum of Modern Art, 1967), 29.

5. Aristotle, *The Poetics* of Aristotle, trans. Preston H. Epps (Chapel Hill: University of North Carolina Press, 1942), 9.

6. Aristotle, *Poetics*, 20.

7. Aristotle, *Poetics*, 18.

8. A. C. Bradley, *Shakespearean Tragedy* (New York: Penguin Books, 1991), 38.

9. Aristotle, *Poetics*, 21.

10. For easy reference to this scene, see the 1962 Atheneum edition of *Who's Afraid of Virginia Woolf?* (p. 179–180), or any of over thirty-five anthologies plus single editions of the play published in the past forty years.

11. *The Collected Works of Samuel Taylor Coleridge, Biographia Literaria, or Biographical Sketches of My Literary Life and Opinions II*, ed. James Engell and W. Jackson Bate (Princeton, NJ: Princeton University Press, 1983), 6.

12. Aristotle, *Poetics*, 30.

13. William Shakespeare, *Romeo and Juliet, A New Variorum Edition*, ed. Horace Furness (New York: Dover Publications, 1963), 293n.

Character

If someone asked you, "Who is this Macbeth?" would you say, "He's Scottish and a nobleman, late twenties, red hair, about five-six or -seven, weighing about 175"? If you were asked, "How about Chief Brody? Who's he?" would you respond, "he's the new chief of police, married, two kids, wears glasses, afraid of the water, which is kind of a hoot since Amity's a beach resort"?

All of this information is relevant, but none of it, in and of itself, communicates who these people are. That's because in both real life and drama, the *essential nature* of a person is revealed not by her mental, physical, biological, psychological, and social *characteristics*, but by *her actions* in pursuit of an objective, which will result in tangible consequences.

Why action? Because talk is cheap. Mary can say she's generous, or people can describe her as such, but until she actually gives something— money, kindness—to someone needy, the truth of this claim will remain conjecture. Furthermore, actions taken when nothing is at stake reveal very

THE RESULT OF ACTION

The most important of these [the constituent elements] is the arrangement of the incidents of the plot; for [drama] is not the portrayal of men [as such], but of action, of life. Happiness and misery are the result of action, and the end [of life (?)] is a certain kind of action and not a quality. Men are the certain kinds of individuals they are as a result of their character; but they become happy or miserable as a result of their actions. Consequently, dramatists do not employ action in order to achieve character portrayal, but they include character because of its relation to action. Therefore, the incidents and plot constitute the end of tragedy, and the end is the greatest thing of all.

Aristotle, *Poetics*, 13.

little about Mary's character, that is, her true nature. If she is rich and shells out a buck or two to a street person, we mutter, "Big deal!" But, if she is a young woman with an average income who has taken a genuine interest in a homeless family and wants to help them, goes to the bank and draws out her savings of $15,000, and gives it to them as a jumpstart fund, we think of her as having a generous and loving nature.

We could probably summarize right now and simply say: the character of a fictional person in a play or film is judged by her actions. The role is characterized by an objective analysis of what the author says about the person in stage directions, about what others say about her, and what she says about herself. External evidence can be used if the person is based on a historical figure. But keep in mind that there is a difference between the actual person and the fictionalized one.

Character—the second of five architectural components of dramatic storytelling we will be discussing in this book—differs from characterization and needs a bit of explaining.

When Hamlet risks his life to follow the ghost and threatens his comrades if they try to stop him; when Macbeth agrees to fight Macduff, even though he knows the witches' prophesies are against him; when Chief Brody chooses to go out on the boat in pursuit of the shark in spite of his fear of the water, the true essence of these characters is being revealed. In all three cases, whatever else may be said about the character of these men, *their actions* demonstrate that they are *brave*.

THE SOUL OF TRAGEDY

The first principle and, as it were, the soul of tragedy is the plot. The second is the character [indicants]. It is the same also in painting; for if anyone should make a painting by smearing the most beautiful colors at random on a surface his painting would not give as much pleasure as a [mere] figure done in outline. Tragedy is an imitation of action, and is for that reason principally concerned with characters in action.

Aristotle, *Poetics*, 14.

Indeed, actions do not lie. We can listen to dialogue about how wonderful a person is and then see him—played by angelic-faced Macaulay Culkin—and instantly believe that he is the kindliest young man in the world. But if, after his girlfriend leaves the room, he kicks her brown-eyed, cocker spaniel puppy, such an action tells us more than any words about his true nature. He is a mean S.O.B!

We will judge a character in a dramatic story by her actions and use adjectives to convey our impressions: avaricious, conscious, considerate, duplicitous, deceitful, evenhanded, generous, greedy, heroic, brave, imaginative, intelligent, levelheaded, loyal, magnanimous, forgiving, malicious, selfish, sensitive, steadfast, stingy, trustworthy, or thousands more. This is how we define true character.

* * *

When Aristotle speaks of character as second of the constituent elements (plot, character, thought, diction, music, and spectacle) of a tragedy, he is speaking of the *essential nature*, which is determined by a fictional person's actions. That's the definition we will use. There are also characteristics to describe the mental, physical, biological, psychological, social, etc., features or qualities of a person. An understanding of this distinction (which may be unique to drama) will tell us why in dramatic storytelling we focus on *actions*: a person struggling to achieve the beat, scene, and act objectives that feed the role's through-line objective. Actions, of course, are choices. Directors, acting teachers, and actors use the word "choice" a great deal. The meaning given in the *Poetics* and the meaning in acting classes and rehearsals is the same: character is revealed through action, and thinking is what leads to action.

We state these—hopefully, clear and simple—definitions up front. If you go to the dictionary and look up "character," you will find the quantity of information could literally fill a page. We tried it as a text box and abandoned the idea because it was a mind-boggler, resulting only in confusion. The major problem is that very few people think of the word *character* as meaning the *essential nature* of the *dramatic persona*—fictional people in

CHARACTER

1) Aristotle's definition of the character:"It is *the situation* of the man of much glory and good fortune" emphasizes the fact that character can only be discussed in context of the plot. A character makes a choice (preconceived by the author), acts upon that choice, and the choice and resulting action reveals the character of the individual.

2) He says that [dramatic storytelling] "is an imitation of an action being carried out by certain individuals who must be certain kinds of persons in character and in thinking—the two criteria by which we determine the quality of an action ...and it is because of these that all men fail or succeed."

3) The word thinking is an attempt to translate the Greek word *dianoia*. Aristotle seemed to mean:"(1) intellectual deliberative capacity; (2) the process of thinking; and (3) the thoughts one gives assent to and acts upon." In short, what are called decisions in the scenes of crisis in the plot section of this book and what acting teachers mean when they say that acting is thinking. He goes on to say that by character he means "that by which we determine what kinds of men are being presented; and by "one's thinking" he means "...that which manifests itself in all the characters."

4) Concerning a character's thoughts, Aristotle notes that they should be "(1) possible [within the limits of the situation] and (2) ...fitting." A character's thinking makes clear a person's choice—what sorts of things he chooses or avoids.

Most directors, acting teachers, and actors use the word choice a great deal. The meaning given in the *Poetics* and the meaning in present day acting classes and rehearsals is the same: character is revealed through action *and thinking*. Decision-making is an action.

Aristotle, *Poetics*, 24, 12, 13, and 14.

---

a film or play. Instead, they use the word to mean the role being played, as in "the character of Jack Twist is played by Jake Gyllenhaal."

An excellent illustration of the distinction between characteristics and true "character" can be found in the opening monologue to Shakespeare's *Richard III*. Richard spends the first half of the speech describing his physical appearance: As a "deformed" and "unfinished" hunchback, he is "not shaped for sportive tricks," nor "made to court an amorous looking glass." Nature has cheated him out of a "fair proportion" and left him so "lamely and unfashionable" that dogs bark at him.

These *characteristics* distinguish him from other people who do not suffer from such physical handicaps. But they do not, in and of themselves, describe his *character*. There are, after all, no meaningful actions inherent in being a hunchback. Such a person might rob a bank or join the Peace Corps, become a barroom brawler or take a monastic vow of lifelong contemplation.

Shakespeare, of course, was far too savvy to rely on such characteristics to inform his audience of Richard's essential nature. Immediately after Richard finishes his self-description, we see his true character emerge as he decides to take his revenge on the world.

> And therefore, since I cannot prove a lover,
> To entertain these fair well-spoken days,
> I am determined to prove a villain
> And hate the idle pleasures of these days.
> Plots have I laid, inductions dangerous,
> By drunken prophecies, libels and dreams,
> To set my brother Clarence and the king
> In deadly hate the one against the other:
> And if King Edward be as true and just
> As I am subtle, false, and treacherous,
> This day should Clarence closely be mew'd up,
> About a prophecy, which says that 'G'
> Of Edward's heirs the murderer shall be.
> Dive, thoughts, down to my soul: here
> Clarence comes.

Because he is a hunchback, he is going to embark on a particular course of *action*, plotting against both his king and his brother in an attempt to seize the throne, an objective he will ultimately risk his life to obtain. This action provides a window into the man's very soul. Now we are able to take a fuller measure of his character, which will shape the plot.

After this speech, if someone asked us, "Who is Richard III?" we would not be content to simply say, "He's an English hunchback nobleman." These characteristics, while true, do not capture his essence as a lying, malicious, and evil man who believes that any means justifies the end and will stop at nothing to get what he wants. And we know this, not just because he says it, but also because *his actions*, throughout the play, confirm it.

All of this is not, however, to say that his characteristic traits are unimportant. They are essential to the degree that they help create a framework, or context, within which the actions that reveal character can believably be undertaken. In short, the traits of the person portrayed must *credibly* lead to the actions that reveal their true nature.

Have you ever left a movie thinking, "Come on, a guy like him would never have done that!"? If so, then you have known a disconnect between characteristics and character. True, the relationship between the two is, to some extent, within the mind of the beholder, since what seems a credible action to one person may not seem convincing to another. But this is no more than to say that the process of evaluating the truth of a story is a subjective one. It is important to understand that *unity of interpretation* should be the goal of theater rehearsals and pre-production meetings in filming.

Characteristic traits are also of benefit to actors who focus on them as a way of finding the character of the person they're portraying. Seemingly insignificant characteristics may stimulate an actor to locate the deeper, inner drives that motivate action. An actor working on a Woody Allen film asked if he could grow a goatee for his character. "Will it help you?" Allen asked. "Yes," the actor replied. "Then do it," said Allen.[1] Clearly, he felt that having a goatee would *not* be contrary to the play's plot, nor the role, nor the time, nor place of the action. So if a goatee helps free some impulse in the actor that leads to action, then it's worth growing the goatee.

Much has been made of Laurence Olivier's fascination with physical characteristics. He famously explained how he liked to start work on a role by building a putty nose. In his autobiography, he says, "I discovered the protective shelter of nose-putty and enjoyed a pleasurable sense of relief and relaxation when some role called for a sculptural addition to my face …enabling me to avoid anything so embarrassing as self-representation."[2] It would seem, then, that it was not so much the search for a role's essential nature that motivated him, but the need to hide some part of himself in order to create the character. And it *is* possible that being in a different place—away from the security of the familiar—expands one's senses and makes an actor more vulnerable to the essential nature of the person she is playing.

As we have noted, we learn about a person's characteristics by what others say about her and by what she says about herself (although both may reflect bias), as well as the author's parenthetical description in the text, which usually precedes her entrance and which we can take as fact.

A good example is Eugene O'Neill's description of Edmund in *A Long Day's Journey into Night*:

> Edmund is ten years younger than his brother [who is 33], a couple of inches taller, thin and wiry. Where Jamie takes after his father, with little resemblance to his mother, Edmund looks like both his parents, but is more like his mother. Her big, dark eyes are the dominant feature in his long, narrow Irish face. His mouth has the same quality of hypersensitiveness hers possesses. His high forehead is hers accentuated, with dark brown hair, sun-bleached to red at the ends, brushed straight back from it. But his nose is his father's and his face in profile recalls Tyrone's. Edmund's hands are noticeably like his mother's, with the same exceptionally long fingers. They even have to a minor degree the same nervousness. It is in the quality of extreme nervous sensibility that the likeness of Edmund to his mother is most marked.
>
> He is plainly in bad health. Much thinner than he should be, his eyes appear feverish and his cheeks are sunken. His skin, in spite of being sunburned a deep brown, has a parched sallowness.
>
> He wears a shirt, collar and tie, no coat, old flannel trousers, brown sneakers.

In Jon Klein's, *T Bone N Weasel*, there is no description of character, just as there are no descriptions in the plays of Shakespeare, and little or no description seems to be the trend in play and film writing. But lengthy descriptions were fairly common for dramatists in the late nineteenth and first half of the twentieth century, especially George Bernard Shaw and Eugene O'Neill. The example above by O'Neill was undoubtedly written as an authorial directive on casting. Some directors today, amenable to casting Lear as a weight-challenged woman, might feel such specific direction an infringement upon their creative prerogatives, but how authors see the people they create often has value. It is true that O'Neill mentions nothing about Edmond's true character in his parenthetical comments, but suggesting that actors waste time focusing on them is tossing the baby out with the bath water. Take a creative approach and try to find in these characteristic traits something that could lead to an action that reveals character.

Reread O'Neill's description of Edmund. Does anything strike you that could possibly be used as an action? Clearly, the fact that Edmund has, as we later discover, tuberculosis, can easily be connected to actions by how he moves, sits, talks, or coughs. But how could coughing reveal character? The actor playing the role has many choices: He might cough without covering his mouth to draw attention to himself, which would be inconsiderate or self-pitying, or he might cough as little as possible, only when absolutely necessary, being as inconspicuous as possible, which would be judged as considerate and respectful. Haven't we all experienced people sitting next to us on an airplane who seem to have never thought of covering their mouths when they cough? And don't we judge them as insensitive, ignorant, or uncaring?

What about the author's description of clothing? Isn't what a person wears revealing of character? When Julia Roberts as Erin Brockovich, a divorced mother of three, desperate for a job, shows up at the law office on her first day of work in a tight, low-cut blouse, other employees judge her as deliberately provocative. Yet the audience sees her for what she is: a no-nonsense, independent woman who wears what she feels comfortable in, and we respect her for it and know she's got the right stuff (character) to take on a Big Business that has been polluting a desert California town for decades.

Obviously, Edmund's clothing—"a shirt, collar and tie, no coat, old flannel trousers, [and] brown sneakers"—is not a choice. It's what he has, plus one suit, and his job does not pay much, and his father is a penny pincher. But the way he wears what he has, comfortably with no fuss, tells us that clothing is not a high priority on his list of values, which signals something about his character, doesn't it?

And what about O'Neill's mention of Edmund's long fingers? Long, slender fingers often appear in literature, as well as in life, to conceptualize an artist, musician, or poet. O'Neill himself had such fingers, and Edmund is a prototype of the author. Of course, we know that long fingers do not validate artistry. Tennessee Williams—arguably our greatest poet-playwright—had fingers that were short and stubby. We understand those who are against stereotyping, but we also know that stereotyping can convey a desired and quick first impression, saving time for further plot development.

Edmund's long fingers are a reflection of his mother's "to a minor degree [and reveal] the same nervousness." How can we use this characteristic in a physical action that reveals character? Obviously, we're not suggesting anything like Bette Davis smoking a cigarette. But a subtle nervousness can be displayed if the actor moves and is in the right position onstage. Edmund's long monologue, when he tells of his voyage to South America, takes place as he, his father, and brother, all of whom who have been drinking heavily, are seated at a round table, stage center. His father is seated up-center at the apex of the triangle, and the two sons are seated either stage right or left.

Of all the scenes that give some indication of the characteristic nervousness of Edmund's hands, it seems this would be it. The speech is difficult as it is extremely poetic to the point of being almost out of context with his naturalistic dialogue in the rest of the play. Let us think of a physical action that would best serve to subtly showcase his nervous fingers.

Instead of staying seated at the table (which makes him turn upstage to his father) and across the table from his brother (which makes him profile to the audience), what if Edmund moves to a desk down right (which faces the audience), sits, turns on a gooseneck reading light, removes a diary from a drawer (or possibly a ledger in which he writes), and *reads* the speech about being on the square rigger bound for Buenos Aires?

This action, used by Robert Sean Leonard in the 2003 Broadway production, served two purposes: the character's hands are more visible to the audience and, since the speech is no longer conversational, it takes the curse off its poetic quality. Prior to his crossing to the desk, the nervousness in his hands can help convey the fact that he feels uncomfortable in such close proximity to his father and brother when talking about his writing. This discomfort affects his movement to the desk but, in contrast, we can see it is, for him, a safe place where he often writes and where he feels comfortable. This is undoubtedly the first time he has let anyone hear this piece of writing. Perhaps it is something for a future one-act play that takes place at sea. But, he worries, is it *too* poetic? His father is a famous actor. Will he like it? Does he reveal too much of himself in the play? Near the end, having read facing the audience rather than looking at his father and brother, he feels he must restore the original relationship. So he closes the diary, keeping it in one hand, remembering by heart what he had written, and finishing it as he moves back to the table.

What would all this reveal about Edmund's character? He is an extremely vulnerable young man, shy and sensitive but ultimately courageous, as are all writers at a first reading, yet determined to be a writer and, above all, a truthful and honest one. And during the entire scene his hands are especially revealing. Not only do they reflect his emotions, but they also echo the nervousness of his mother's hands and tell us of their closeness and love as well as the deep empathy of which he is capable.

As a byproduct of this solution to find an action stemming from a characteristic, we are also foreshadowing O'Neill's power as well as his weakness as a dramatist. After Edmund has finished reading, his father says he has the makings of a poet, and Edmund replies, "No, I can only stammer." That also was true of O'Neill, who lacked a certain facility of language; the strength of his poetic sensibility being revealed mostly in his plots and people. The scene also forecasts his mother's final entrance. Having yielded to her addiction, she returns down the stairs to the family and tells of her first meeting with Tyrone; in the telling, her hand movements are almost as important as the words.

There is an instance of an author's written *action* that would clearly reveal character but was ignored in the original Broadway production. In John Patrick Shanley's Pulitzer and Tony award-winning play *Doubt*, Sister Aloysius has a last minute change of character. "Bending with emotion" on her final line, she says, "I have my doubts! I have such doubts!" but both the line and the emotion seem to some viewers to come from the vastness of nothing and seem in conflict with the actions she has taken throughout the play.

What author's direction was left out that might have motivated this last moment change in character and given it believability? When Mrs. Muller exits after her intensely emotional interview with Aloysius, Shanley's stage direction reads: "Sister Aloysius is shaken." There is no place prior to this moment where Aloysius could show she is shaken. In fact, during the interview, she becomes even firmer in her resolve to rid St. Nicholas of Father Flynn because she finds she cannot rely on Mrs. Muller as an ally.

Shanley then writes, "Flynn appears at the door. He's in a controlled fury." In performance, this entrance took place before the actor playing Aloysius could start to act "being shaken." We take it that "being shaken" means that her rigid position regarding Flynn is somewhat neutralized by Mrs. Muller's plea to allow the priest to stay. If this action had not been eliminated by the quick entrance of Father Flynn, it would have given the audience insight into Aloysius' true nature, revealing her not just as a one-dimensional zealot out to get Flynn but as a more compassionate woman. This, in turn, would have provided her a measure of believability, understanding, and sympathy at the play's end.

* * *

We mentioned earlier that what people say about themselves is not always the best indicator of their true character. Why? Because characters, like people in real life, have too strong an incentive to speak falsely about themselves to get what they want. A perfect and humorous example of this dynamic is found in Howard Korder's *Boy's Life*. In one scene, Jack, one of the leading characters of the story, is trying to pick up a young woman, Maggie, who sits next to him on a park bench. After she rebuffs his first attempts at conversation, he notices she is wearing a decorative button and decides this is the opening he is looking for:

> JACK: You know—excuse me—that's a bad place for a button. It can restrict your circulation. Should I take if off?
>
> MAGGIE: Where'd you get that?
>
> JACK: I beg your pardon, but I didn't "get it" anywhere. It's something I have to know in my line of work.
>
> MAGGIE: And what might that be?
>
> JACK: I'm a cardiologist. (Pause.)
>
> MAGGIE: Please go away.

Later in the scene, Maggie challenges Jack's description of himself:

> MAGGIE: You're not really a cardiologist.
>
> JACK: Not literally, no.

Both of these characterizations cannot be true. It's easy to detect Jack's motivation for lying. What better way to impress Maggie than to make her think he is a high-status, well-paid professional? If his objective is to get her to come back to his place—which, by the end of the scene, is made perfectly clear—this tactic might very well serve. Looking at the scene not through verbal characterization but through objective and action, it's a pretty safe bet to assume he's not a heart doctor.

So what do these exchanges reveal about Jack's true character? That he is willing to both flagrantly lie and sheepishly confess his lying if he thinks either tactic will help get a woman into bed. Are these actions not worth a thousand descriptions of his height or religion or finger length? Well, yes, but the absence of any physical descriptions does tell us something. Unlike O'Neill, Korder is saying that, in casting this role, no specific characterizations are important. Any fairly young, male actor with a sense of comedy could play Jack.

* * *

In many stories, as in life itself, the true character of a person changes through the events encountered and the actions taken. A character may begin a play or film as one kind of person, and end up another. Indeed, this transformation of character—the affirmation of the idea that people *can* change—is one of the great pleasures of drama.

In *The African Queen*, Charlie Allnut transforms himself into a man profoundly at odds with both his characterization and his character at the film's beginning. When the story starts, Charlie is the Canadian captain and crew of a small steam launch, *The African Queen*, plying the Congo River at the onset of World War I. Boozy, uncouth, and unshaven, he seems as decrepit as his boat. Untouched by the approaching conflict, he seems more interested in drinking gin, the pleasures of the flesh, and ministering to his boat's leaky engine than in risking his life for a mother country he left and a war he knows nothing about. If we were to judge his character at this point, we'd say he was self-centered, not particularly courageous, nor governed by any high-minded ideals or principles.

Into his life comes Rosie Sayer, the sister of an English missionary. After German solders kill her brother, she decides to use Charlie's boat to exact revenge by sinking a German ship downriver. Not surprisingly, Charlie initially balks at the scheme. As mentioned earlier, there is a plenitude of obstacles to such a plan—rapids, crocodiles, a German fort, the bristling guns of the target ship itself—and nothing in either Charlie's appearance or conduct, when we first encounter him, would lead us to conclude that he is the kind of character for such a mission.

But he changes as the story progresses, finding the strength to overcome all obstacles. He is willing to brave German gunfire, leeches, and a storm-tossed lake to reach their goal. Through his actions, we see him transformed from a walking gin-blossom into a hero. By the drama's end, we feel he has more than earned Rosie's assessment of him: "You're the bravest man that ever lived."

An example in which a characteristic given in dialogue is *not* presented *through actions* is found in the film *Jaws*. One aspect of Brody's character is his fear of the water. This is *talked about* four times in the film. The first is when an old geezer comes up to Brody on the beach and, referring to the water, says, "It's cold. We know all about you, Chief. You don't go in the water at all, do you?" to which the Chief replies, "It's some bad hat, Harry." This dialogue is almost impossible to connect to hydrophobia since no mention of it is made prior to this exchange.

Also, one really has to watch the film more than once before realizing that the old geezer with a wicked Scandinavian accent is the same man who, minutes before, is momentarily viewed by Brody surfacing from the water in a black bathing cap. Brody, and we, at first think the hat is the dorsal fin of a shark. The dramatic form is ephemeral. It is not the same as reading a book, where, if you don't understand something, you can turn back and reread, connecting the dots. Identifying this surfacing man, whose face we see only momentarily, with the man who approaches Brody takes some doing and does not serve to reveal Brody's character whatsoever.

The next reference to Brody's hydrophobia comes when Hooper visits the Chief's household the evening after the mother of the young boy—the story's second shark victim—has slapped Brody because she found out that he knew of the shark's presence and kept the beaches open.

Brody has not yet told his wife that the shark the town's crazies caught may *not*, according to Hooper, be the same one that killed the woman's son. As he sits brooding about his complicity in the young boy's death, Hooper arrives with a couple of bottles of wine. The conversation between Brody's wife and Hooper is as follows: "Martin hates boats," she says, touching her husband's arm. "Martin hates water. Martin sits in his car when we go on the ferry to the mainland. I guess it's a childhood thing. There's a clinical name for it, isn't there?"

"Drowning," Brody answers.

The lines spoken by the wife are barely audible due to a lack of vocal projection plus poor enunciation. The shot pictures Brody, sitting at the table, in the center of the frame; Hooper seated to his right (as viewed from the audience); and the wife seated on his left but closer to the camera than Brody. Consequently, she delivers the line with her back three-quarters to the viewers.

Immediately following this scene, the two men are on the dock and Brody is cutting the shark open. Since sharks have a slow digestive system, Hooper knows that if this indeed *is* the shark responsible for killing the young boy, his remains will be in the shark's stomach. They are not.

Since the shark is a night feeder, Hooper says they will go out in his boat and look for it.

"I'm not going in a glass boat," Brody says.

"Yes, you are," replies Hooper.

"No I'm not."

"Yes, you are."

"I can't do that," Brody insists.

"Yes, you can."

The next shot shows them out at sea. Brody, fortified with Dutch courage, the bottle of wine in his hand, has slightly slurred speech. Later in the scene, Hooper says, "It doesn't make sense. A guy who hates water to live on an island."

All of the above is in dialogue form and could signal characterization if *it could be understood* in the setup scene by the wife's dialogue. Actions, however, speak louder than words. If this phobia is really important to the story, there is no scene *in action* that illustrates Brody's fear. As you can see from the next text box, in the novel most of this information is presented as *subjective thinking*, so it serves the purpose of informing the reader. But without an action scene, showing his fear, this characteristic serves no useful purpose. Our guess is that, except for the above dialogue, this aspect of Brody's character was eliminated. How can the actor playing Brody play a subjective obstacle, or even an objective obstacle, if there is no scene dramatizing his fear of the water?

If you are working on a film or a play that deals with historical characters, you can research characteristics of the person. There have been a plethora of one-person works based on characters such as Mark Twain,

---

SLIMY, SAVAGE THINGS

Brody felt a shimmer of fear skitter up his back. He was a very poor swimmer, and the prospect of being on top of—let alone in—water above his head gave him what his mother used to call the wimwams: sweaty palms, a persistent need to swallow, and an ache in his stomach, essentially the sensation some people feel about flying. In Brody's dreams, deep water was populated by slimy, savage things that rose from below and shredded his flesh, by demons that cackled and moaned.

* * *

Don't be stupid! I'm not willing to get killed. I'm not even willing—that's the word you want to use—to go out in that goddamn boat. You think I like it out there? I'm so scared every minute I'm out there, I want to puke.

* * *

We're sinking, he told himself, and the memories of his childhood nightmares leaped into his mind.

Peter Benchley, *Jaws* (New York: Bantam Books, 1975), 78, 293, and 305.

Lyndon Johnson, Ethel Merman, Lillian Hellman, Virginia Woolf, Colette, Emily Dickenson, Isak Dinesen, and others. And how about such films as *The Queen* (Elizabeth II), *The Aviator* (Howard Hughes), *Ray* (Ray Charles), *Walk the Line* (Johnny Cash), *Capote, Gandhi, Amadeus, Pride of the Yankees* (Lou Gehrig), and documentaries such as *Grizzly Man* (Timothy Treadwell)?

And what of illustrations? One could not think of a production of *Alice in Wonderland* that ignored Sir John Tenniel's drawings of Alice, the Mad Hatter, the Duchess, the White Rabbit, etc. You might decide not to use them, but you certainly should look at them. These illustrations depend on caricature, which exaggerates or distorts the characters' distinctive features and peculiarities to produce a comic effect. You can learn a lot about characters from such illustrations.

POET AND HISTORIAN

The difference between a poet and a historian is this: the historian relates what has happened, the poet what could happen. Therefore, poetry is something more philosophic and of more serious import than history; for poetry tends to deal with the general, while history is concerned with delimited particular facts.

Aristotle, *Poetics,* 18.

You can also aid your delineation of character by either pictures (paintings, drawings, or photographs) or writings about historical figures.

There are cases, however, where exhaustive research on the actual historical figure may prove counterproductive because the author has fictionalized a real person—whose through-line objective supports the author's theme—but is only partially based on the actual historical figure. Historical evidence that pictures the actual person, then, could upset the fictional balance of the play or film and its meaning. There is a difference in purpose between history and poetry (see text box above).

Further, it may depend upon the actors' method of working as to whether or not they want to research the historical background. Many actors have written or been interviewed about this matter, but what they have to say seems a reiteration of what two actors, Paul Muni and Raymond Massey, both stage and film actors, said on the matter many years ago. Muni, who loved to research the character, said:

> If my story is biographical, I try to get photographs or paintings of the character. Then I read as much of the background material as is available: books which explain his life and times to me, and those materials which give me his mental world. For Zola, there was everything: photographs, his books, what his contemporaries wrote about him and the photostats of the court records in the Dreyfus case.[3]

Raymond Massey, however, had a contrary point of view:

> Again and again I am asked the question: how much research should an actor do in preparing his part? While getting ready for Robert

Sherwood's *Abe Lincoln in Illinois* ...I deliberately avoided more than a cursory research. The deep study of Lincoln which Mr. Sherwood had made supplied me with a wealth of relevant material which an author of his genius and theatrical knowledge considered sufficient—and *not more* than sufficient ...for developing the character. Over-embellishment—a satiety of detail—might have seriously jeopardized in performance a figure which the author had conceived in superb economy and sincerity.[4]

Massey explains that there are dangers in research. Not only did he talk to people who knew Lincoln, but he also read the Herndon letters and many other sources about Lincoln and found his voice to be "shrill, raucous, high-pitched" and that he spoke with a "staccato nervousness." He also found Lincoln's voice described as "deep and resonant" and that he spoke with a "slow drawl." He discovered that Lincoln moved with "the panther grace of an Indian" and that he moved with "quick steps." Massey says that he eventually "threw aside" all the information "in favor of a physical delineation which [he] considered most theatrically effective to project Mr. Sherwood's Lincoln."[5]

* * *

One final point: analyzing character—through action—helps us to lay to rest the age-old conflict over the relative importance of character versus plot. Aristotle famously placed plot at the top of the great chain of dramatic being. The "soul of tragedy," he called it.[6] Second on his list was character. But, in truth, the two are inseparably connected, for it is only through the selection of events that constitute the plot that the characters are forced to make the choices and take the actions that reveal their true selves. Character cannot be expressed in any other way. Likewise, a drama whose plot structure doesn't force a character into these choices and actions will, in addition to boring the audience, shine little light on any of the elusive mysteries of human existence that draw us to the dramatic arts in the first place.

To summarize: Character is best projected to the audience *through actions* dramatized in the beats, scenes, acts, and the play as a whole.

Characteristics of the *dramatis personæ* are also important, especially as they suggest action. Such characteristics, however, are very often emphasized at the expense of actions for evaluating character. We urge practitioners and fans alike to reassess this imbalance toward a view of favoring an analysis of character *through actions* as the essential requirement for stage and screen.

Notes

1. This story was told to co-author, David Letwin, by a friend, Matt Servitto, the actor involved. If personal citing is difficult for you to understand, think of it this way: *If* the story was fictitious, would the point made be less truthful—i.e., if something is not contrary to time or place, but aids the actor in his process of creating the character, it's OK? Check out the "Poet and Historian" text box in this chapter.

2. Laurence Olivier, *Confessions of an Actor, an Autobiography* (New York: Simon and Schuster, 1982), 38.

3. Toby Cole and Helen Krich Chinoy, eds., *Actors on Acting: The Theories, Techniques and Practices of the World's Great Actors, Told in Their Own Words* (New York: Crown Publishers, Inc., 1960), 527.

4. Cole and Chinoy, *Actors on Acting*, 533–534.

5. Cole and Chinoy, *Actors on Acting*, 535.

6. Aristotle, *Poetics*, 14.

Theme

The two architectural components we have so far discussed—plot and character—ultimately serve to express a drama's third component: its theme, by which we mean the *author's point of view* on the subject matter.

Under the definition of "subject," the dictionary lists "theme" as a synonym—go figure!—and, while we admit these words are often used interchangeably, we are making a distinction between them. We interpret the subject of *Jaws* as survival; the subject of *Macbeth* as vaulting ambition. But the true meaning of these dramas goes far beyond these objective descriptions. It is found in the author's perspective on these topics as subjectively interpreted by the practitioners involved in production. What does *Jaws* illustrate about survival? What is Shakespeare saying about excessive ambition? Answer these questions and you are getting to the center of the story.

SUPER-OBJECTIVE

Stanislavsky warned against choosing a super-objective that is merely theatrical or perfunctory and urged that one be chosen that is human and directed toward the accomplishment of the basic purpose of the play. He analogizes the super-objection to a main artery, providing nourishment and life . . . to the production, guiding the artists from the beginning to the end, and galvanizing the units and objectives. He said that what is needed is a super-objective in harmony with the intentions of the playwright and one that arouses a response in the soul. Search for it, he suggests, not only in the play but in the [artists] themselves.

Constantin Stanislavsky, *An Actor Prepares*, trans. Elizabeth Reynolds Hapgood (New York: Theatre Arts Books, 1936), 284.

The very process of selectivity, common to all dramatic storytellers, guarantees a point of view. The writer's perspective is clarified and illuminated by the choice of events, characters, and environment, which relate to the subject. Since there is this absolute organic connection between a story's plot and its point of view, practitioners should first discuss and decide together on their interpretation of the writer's theme and make it resonate with viewers as it must have resonated with whoever selected it for production in the first place. Stanislavsky clearly states that, although creative work is an expression of the artist's subconscious, an understanding of the author's theme—which he called the "super-objective"—is of prime importance because it sets parameters and, therefore, is a *means* into the creative world of the interpreters.

Some view pre-production discussion as antithetical to skills best honed by the doing and redoing until they become second nature. Skills orientation rehearsals focus on blocking and line-memorization. This method may work well for voice production, speech, and movement, but it does not serve the creative process that should be the focus in rehearsals with the director, actors, playwright, and designers. It is thorough discussions, leading to commitment to a theme, that will mark the difference

---

THE COMMON UNIFYING BOND

Dostoyevski was impelled to write . . . by his lifelong search for God, Tolstoy spent his life struggling for self-perfection, and Chekhov wrestled with the triviality of bourgeois life. What gave birth to the creation of the play, Stanislavsky says, should also be the fountainhead for the inspiration of the participating artists. These larger, vital purposes of great writers have the power to focus all of an artist's creative faculties in every beat and scene and the whole stream of individual, minor objectives, all the imaginary thoughts, feelings, and actions. . . . The super-objective, the common unifying bond is so great, that even the most insignificant detail of the production, if it is not related to it, will stand out as superfluous or wrong.

Stanislavsky, *An Actor Prepares*, 356.

between a technically proficient performance and an evening of spirit and fire that only strong commitment can bring.

Earlier, we discussed the relationship of *Jaws'* climax to its theme. At the climax, Chief Brody's decision to blow the shark out of the water, by shooting the compressed air tank into its mouth, comes to fruition. This action encapsulates the story's theme, which should reflect *all* such life-threatening instances. *People will—rightly—go to any lengths to defend their territory—home, family—against whatever threatens it or them.* Most viewers will not only agree but can give some degree of passionate commitment to this point of view by analogizing it to experiences in their own life. They can also look to specific instances, such as territorial disputes (Palestinian/ Israelis), disputes between government and the individual (Roe v. Wade), feuds between neighbors (Hatfields and McCoys), a mother's right to defend her child if she is threatened, robbery, kidnapping, sexual coercion, or in clashes with authorities about eminent domain, and so forth.

Not only in the climax, but also in every element of the story's architecture, theme must be reflected. If *Macbeth* illustrates that unbridled ambition can bring a man "of much glory and good fortune"[1] to his ruin, then this point of view shapes the play's choice of events and characters from start to finish. It is not mere coincidence that Shakespeare has a sergeant in the second scene report on Macbeth's courage and loyalty as displayed in the just-completed battle and has a scene in which King Duncan, overcome with gratitude for Macbeth's service, showers him with rewards.

But driven by vaulting ambition, Macbeth kills the king, orchestrates the murder of his friend Banquo, suffers from guilt-induced hallucinations, loses his wife to suicide, and eventually sinks to such a state of internal dislocation that he feels life is nothing but "a tale / told by an idiot, full of sound and fury, / signifying nothing." Finally, he is slain by Macduff, and his fall is complete. These events and characters do not arise out of thin air but are centrally related to the author's point of view on the subject of unbridled ambition.

This is not to say that a writer necessarily *begins* the creative process by consciously determining the theme—although some do just that. On

5 January 1935, Clifford Odets' *Waiting for Lefty*, about a taxi strike the previous year, opened in New York and turned out to be an event to be noted in the history of American theater. *Lefty* is a propaganda play whose purpose is to rouse the audience into political opposition. The subject is capitalist exploitation; the theme, that workers can overcome their exploitation by taking collective action. Since this play served a desired reaction—to support an actual strike of taxi drivers that had occurred in New York City and by universalizing this to *all* workers exploited by big business interests everywhere—Odets decided his theme at the beginning of the writing process and then orchestrated the plot and the characters around it.

Whether the writer starts with the theme or it comes to her through the writing, at some point during the process of creation, she will most likely hit upon her point of view. If the writer seeks coherence, she will want all the architectural components and structural parts of plot to fit within

WAITING FOR LEFTY

The first scene of [*Waiting for Lefty*] had not played two minutes when a shock of delighted recognition struck the audience like a title wave. Deep laughter, hot assent, a kind of joyous fervor seemed to sweep the audience toward the stage. The actors no longer performed; they were being carried along as if by an exultance of communication. . . . Audience and actors had become one. Line after line brought applause, whistles, bravos, and heartfelt shouts of kinship. . . . When the audience at the end of the play responded to the militant question from the stage: Well, what's the answer? with a spontaneous roar of Strike! Strike! it was something more than a tribute to the play's effectiveness, more even than a testimony of the audience's hunger for constructive social action. It was the birth cry of the thirties. Our youth had found its voice. It was a call to join the good fight for a greater measure of life in a world free of economic fear, falsehood, and craven servitude to stupidity and greed. Strike! was Lefty's lyric message, not alone for a few extra pennies of wages or the shorter hours of work, strike for greater dignity, strike for a bolder humanity, strike for the full stature of man.

Harold Clurman, *The Fervent Years: The Story of the Group Theatre in the Thirties* (New York and London: Harcourt, Brace and Jovanovich, 1975), 147–148.

that theme, whatever it may be. Robert McKee relates the story of visiting the legendary screenwriter Paddy Chayefsky, noting that he had a strip of paper taped to the wall several inches above his typewriter. On the paper was a single handwritten sentence. McKee asked him what the sentence meant and why it was taped to the wall. Chayefsky explained that it contained the theme of the story he was working on, and he taped it above his typewriter to make sure that nothing that wasn't connected to that theme made its way into the typewriter![2]

In contrast to Stanislavsky's view that the analysis of theme sets parameters and focus necessary for the creative process of rehearsals, many artists—writers especially—hate talking about the theme of their work and go so far as to reject point of view altogether. When someone asks "What does it mean?" they sometimes shout: "It doesn't *mean* anything. It just is!"

This reaction probably results from the distrust they have of intellectual analysis, which they think of as post-creative. The truth for them lies in the interior regions of the subconscious. They fear that if they dissect the theme, either before or during the creative process, the mystery and value of the work will disappear.

They may have a point. It is *after* their creation is completed that they want an informal reading of their initial efforts followed by a discussion. The same is true in acting, which, like writing, is a *creative* act. But, as with

---

THE UNCONSCIOUS

Playwright Edward Albee feels that his imaginative powers come from his unconscious, and that they must be protected from consciousness lest they wither and harden, like underwater plants exposed to air. He dislikes explaining his writing process or the origin of his ideas, even to himself. "I don't consider myself an intellectual," he says. "I'm not sure that I think coherently terribly well." He defers to his unconscious in most things because it knows more than he does.

Larissa MacFarquhar, "Profile of Albee," *The New Yorker* (April 4, 2005): 68–77.

"IT IS SHAMEFUL TO LIVE LIKE THAT"

Chekhov's subject is the Russian people, or more universally, humanity. His theme, the tone of which is humorously gentle and scientifically objective, is, "You live badly, my friends. It is shameful to live like that." This point of view implies that people should live better, more productive lives.

*   *   *

In speaking to a young, would-be writer, Chekhov said: "You say that you have wept over my plays. Yes, and not only you alone. But I did not write them for this purpose, it is Alekseev [Stanislavsky] who has made such crybabies of them. I desired something other. I only wished to tell people honestly: Look at yourselves, see how badly and boringly you live! The only principal thing is that people should understand this, and when they do, they will surely create for themselves another and better life. I will not see it, but I know it will be entirely different, not like what we have now. And as long as it does not exist, I'll continue to tell people: See how badly and boringly you live! Is it that which they weep over?"

Alex Kuprin, I. A. Bunin, and Maxim Gorky, *Reminiscences of Anton Chekhov*, trans. S. S. Koteliansky and Leonard Woolf (New York: B. W. Huebsch, 1921), 24; and Ernest J. Simmons, *Chekhov: A Biography* (Chicago: University of Chicago Press, 1962), 58l.

the writer, after actors have worked on a scene and presented it to fellow students, there is always discussion as to its effectiveness. It was as a director, who is also an interpreter, that Stanislavsky felt the need to intellectually isolate the primary artist's theme in order to set parameters and focus on the organic connection between the creator and the creation that would best serve rehearsals and production meetings.

For all of his fame in championing the emotional life of the actor through such means as sense memory and "becoming the character," Stanislavsky saw analysis of the author's theme as *central* to the interpreters' work. Although his legacy abides, in his Method Acting technique as it was manifested in his productions of Chekhov's plays, the playwright often sharply disagreed (see above text box).

Perhaps the only conclusion we can draw is that works of art are not the sole product of either the subconscious or the intellect. Grand ideas and logical discourse, however well articulated, may or may not produce what Tennessee Williams described with admiration as that "disturbing kink in the guts" of the audience.[3] Is it possible that the achievement of the ideal reaction—"Ah, I get it!"—is achieved by individual artists in direct degree to the differences in which they uniquely combine the rational with the subconscious?

Having defined and identified the importance of theme—and the various times in the creative process in which this is done—what exactly, beyond the broad idea of "point of view," do we mean by theme? While there are as many different themes on the subject of human existence as there are artists expressing them, a perusal of the history of dramatic literature leads us to conclude that almost all themes can be examined, to one degree or another, in relationship to the artist's point of view of the possibility, likelihood, and causes of meaningful changes in life. Do people, or the conditions of their existence, change? If so, how and why does this change occur?

For most of human existence, the answer to the question "Does life change?" has been an unqualified "Yes." It is hard to find an example of a drama before the twentieth century in which the characters, the world they inhabit, or both, do not undergo a detectable, meaningful change over the course of the story's telling.

The tragedies of ancient Greece exemplify this dynamic. In *Oedipus Rex*, one of the most famous dramas in all of Western history, King Oedipus is presented as a man of status and power to whom all the citizens of a plague-ravaged Thebes look for protection and succor. He is confident and self-assured. By the end of the play, he is a broken man, blinded by his own hand, banished from the city by his own command, unable to deny that his murderous and incestuous actions have made him the "polluter of the land."

Indeed, this notion of change is at the heart of Aristotle's view of drama: "a general definition of magnitude for an action [i.e., story] would be: that amount of magnitude in which events proceeding in succession according to probability and necessity veer around from bad to good fortune or from good to bad."[4]

This shift in fortune is no less present in our time than it was in classical Greece. Dorothy feels so alienated from her family in *The Wizard of Oz* that she runs away from the Kansas farm to protect her dog, hoping to find self-fulfillment over the rainbow. By the end of the story, she declares, "there's no place like home," and earnestly swears that she will never look for happiness beyond. She has moved from alienation to integration.

In *Jaws*, it is the town itself that undergoes this Aristotelean change of fortune. In the beginning of the film, the community is terrorized by a twenty-five-foot, great white shark; at the end, the threat has been eliminated. In *Death of a Salesman*, Willy Loman is alive at the beginning; he is dead by the end.

Drama seeks to do more, however, than merely present existential change. It also seeks to address how or why these changes occur. If we assume that Oedipus goes through a major transformation from good fortune to bad over the course of the drama, why does this happen? What accounts for his downfall? Something must explain it.

We know that for the Greeks, the notion of *hamartia*, or tragic flaw, was central to the tragic experience. The tragic character is "the situation of the man of much glory and good fortune who is not [too] superior in excellence and uprightness and yet does not come into his misfortune because of baseness and rascality but through some inadequacy or positive fault."[5] How that flaw would be characterized in the case of Oedipus is, of course, open to interpretation; many have argued it is his pride and arrogance. But whatever practitioners decide on, the theme of Sophocles' work is that this flaw causes the change of fortune undergone by its leading character.

Macbeth describes quite clearly his tragic flaw, and thus the agency of his downfall: "vaulting ambition." It is this trait that leads him to take the actions that inexorably change his life for the worse. Shakespeare has directed all his creative energies to illustrating the theme that over-reaching ambition leads to physical and spiritual dissolution. If the creative artists knowingly violate that theme by attempting to illustrate its oppo-site, in what way is the production still Shakespeare's *Macbeth*?

The Theme of *A Streetcar Named Desire*

It is entirely possible that a given drama may suggest a different theme to different practitioners interpreting it. The original Broadway productions of Tennessee Williams's *A Streetcar Named Desire*, directed by Elia Kazan, and the National Company, directed by Harold Clurman—both gifted and intelligent directors—were said to have been performed in diametrically opposite ways. (See accompanying text boxes.)

In discussing the relative merits of Kazan's and Clurman's interpreta-tions, we start with the premise that neither director was interested in self-aggrandizement at the expense of the author's play, but that each interpreted and directed it as best he could in light of his own background, experience, and intellect.

Perhaps Clurman felt freer than Kazan to be critical of American soci-ety after his appearance before the House Committee on Un-American Activities. Or is it possible that there was a difference in sexuality that played a factor in their choice of theme?

Or perhaps based on evidence in the text boxes, Kazan's position was not really as hard-nosed as myth would have it. Perhaps he simply "went with

---

KAZAN ON *STREETCAR*

Harold Clurman directed the road version of the play, [in which Ms. Hagen played Blanche] and he saw the play as almost symbolic, as though Blanche represented culture that was dying, culture being devoured by the aggres-sive, cruel forces around it in American life. He saw Blanche as a heroine. I did-n't. I saw Blanche as Williams, an ambivalent figure who is attracted by the harshness and vulgarity around him at the same time that he fears it, because it threatens his life.

Michael Ciment, *Kazan on Kazan* (New York: The Viking Press, 1974), 71.

ALDER ON *STREETCAR*

A play like *A Streetcar Named Desire* might be interpreted as a plea for the sensitive: the problem of a hypersensitive romantic victim of a brutal society. It may ask the audience for compassion for its victim. In this interpretation, Blanche would be the protagonist of the play; Stanley the antagonist; Stella fluctuating and caught between; Mitch, beginning by joining with the protagonist, but ending up against her; the poker players siding with the antagonist; the newsboy with the protagonist; and the neighbors caught between. You could immediately have sides for and against, consequently the rudiments of necessary basic relationships of the characters—not only to the play but to each other. In fact, the play was produced with this theme. The play has also been produced as a plea for a down-to-earth, rational life by a director who envisioned a healthy, animal society represented by Stella and Stanley and their friends. Into this society a highly destructive and neurotic Blanche enters from a sick world of the past to destroy this functioning society, undermining the very fiber of Stella's and Stanley's lives. Consequently, the relationships of the characters to the play and to each other become diametrically opposed.

Uta Hagen, *Respect for Acting* (New York: MacMillan, 1973), 148.

the money," since Williams was happy with the acting: a highly sexually-charged, charismatic performance by Marlon Brando, opposite English trained Jessica Tandy, who was said to be more rigid in her acting method.

In deciding which interpretation the reader will choose, it might be wise to start with an analysis of the organic relationship between theme and the plot's structural parts.

With Stanley as the leading character, the inciting incident comes in scene 4 (page 70 of 142 pages), when he overhears Blanche telling Stella that he is "common" and "bestial" and compares him to an ape. His objective is to protect his lair by getting rid of Blanche or by getting back at her. In either case, the obstacles are his wife's loyalty to her sister, Blanche's strength as an antagonist, and his lack of a concrete plan.

When he makes his crisis decision is uncertain, but in scene 8, Blanche's birthday party, he gives her a present—a one-way ticket back to

"MARLON IS A GENIUS"

On stage in New Haven and even more in Boston, Brando seemed, in Kazan's view, to overwhelm Jessica Tandy theatrically. The director wondered if something essentially in the balance of the performance had gone wrong.....Kazan worried that audiences favored Brando; Tennessee cared not at all....Kazan brought up his concern about the imbalance on stage between Tandy and Brando. "She'll get better," Tennessee said. "Blanche is not an angel without a flaw ... and Stanley's not evil. I know you're used to clearly stated themes, but this play should not be loaded one way or the other. Don't try to simplify things. ...Go on working as you are. Marlon is a genius, but she's a worker and she will be better. And better.

Elia Kazan, *A Life* (New York: Knopf, 1988), 346.

Laurel, Mississippi. He justifies this action by informing Stella, in the previous scene, of Blanche's past. His intention is to protect his buddy, Mitch, from marrying such a woman.

You might wish to place the crisis in scene 10, when Stanley makes his decision to rape Blanche. "He stares at [Blanche] for a count of ten. Then a clicking becomes audible from the telephone, steady and rasping. Stanley: You left th' phone off th' hook. (He crosses to it deliberately and sets it back on the hook.)" After he has replaced it, he stares at her again, "his mouth slowly curving into a grin," and just a bit later says, "Come to think of it—maybe you wouldn't be bad—to interfere with." In either choice, you have the completion of his objective and his through-line of action.

In the latter choice, the climax is the rape (about thirty seconds of stage time), and the resolution of the play, scene 11, involves Blanche's preparation for departure, the poker game, the arrival of the doctor and nurse, Blanche's struggle and subjugation, and Stanley's comforting Stella by kneeling beside her and putting his fingers down the opening of her blouse.

On the other hand, if we take Blanche as the leading character, the inciting incident occurs when the high school superintendent calls Blanche into his office and fires her some weeks prior to the opening of the play.

"EMPTY AS A DILETTANTE'S DISCOURSE"

Jessica Tandy's Blanche suffers from the actress' narrow emotional range ... [and then much further on in the review, she] is fragile without being touching. [Her] speeches—which are lovely in themselves—sound phony, and her long words and noble appeals are as empty as a dilettantes discourse because they do not flow from the spring of warm feeling which is the justification and essence of Blanche's character.

Harold Clurman, *The Collected Works of Harold Clurman*, ed. Marjorie Loggia and Glenn Young (New York: Applause Books, 1994), 133.

Her specific objective is to go to New Orleans to visit her sister and find a man to marry—"a cleft in the rock of the world that [she] can hide in." Her obstacles, aside from the formidable Stanley, are the French Quarter—a not very conducive place to find the kind of man she wants to marry—her age, her background of alleged sexual promiscuity after her young husband Alan Gray killed himself, and the time and place. What

"WE THREW THE PLAY OFF BALANCE"

Brando: I think Jessica and I were both miscast, and between us we threw the play out of balance. Jessica is a very good actress, but I never thought she was believable as Blanche. I didn't think she had the finesse or cultivated femininity that the part required, nor the fragility that Tennessee envisioned.... I think Jessica could have made Blanche a truly pathetic person, but she was too shrill to elicit the sympathy and pity that the woman deserved. Because it was out of balance, people laughed at me at several points in the play, turning Blanche into a foolish character, which was never Tennessee's intention. I didn't try to make Stanley funny. People simply laughed, and Jessica was furious because of this, so angry that she asked Gadge [Kazan] to fix it somehow, which he never did. I saw a flash of resentment in her every time the audience laughed at me. She really disliked me for it.

Sam Staggs, *When Blanche Met Brando* (New York: St. Martin's Press, 2005), 91.

occupation was there for an unmarried Southern woman in the mid-1940s other than teacher, nurse, secretary, or housewife?

Her crisis scene, in which she makes a final decision so that she can remain free to pursue her objective, is when she steps out onto the porch, sees the doctor, and stops short. Frightened, she whispers, "That man is not Shep Huntleigh." Avoiding the poker players, she goes into the bedroom. "Lurid reflections" appear on the walls, the "Varsouviana" plays in her mind. She is approached by the Matron and Stanley, who tears the lantern off the light bulb. Blanche breaks past the Matron, who catches hold of her arm. She turns wildly and scratches at the Matron as she pinions her arms. Blanche falls to her knees.

While this is going on, Eunice takes care of a distraught Stella. Mitch crosses toward the bedroom to protect Blanche, but Stanley pushes him back. All of this action is the climax. Blanche's giving up her struggle and being led out by the doctor is the resolution.

We would lean heavily toward Blanche as the leading character because Stanley's through-line objective is not decided upon until halfway through the play, in scene 8, or, if you chose the rape scene as the crisis and climax, scene 10.

It has been argued that Stanley is thrown out of adjustment when Blanche first arrives. Is he? She becomes ill at the end of the scene because of her feelings of guilt for saying "I know, you disgust me" to her young husband

---

"THAT AWFUL WOMAN"

[Kazan speaking about opening night in Boston] Louis B. Mayer, [Hollywood Studio Boss and father of Irene Mayer Selznick, Producer of *Streetcar*] "urged me to make the author do one critically important bit of rewriting to make sure that once that awful woman who'd come to break up that fine young couple's happy home was packed off to an institution, the audience would believe that the young couple would live happily ever after." It never occurred to him that Tennessee's primary sympathy was with Blanche.

Elia Kazan, *A Life* (New York: Knopf, 1988), 345.

before he killed himself; or perhaps because of her realization of her sexual attraction for Stanley. But he is not the least bit out of adjustment.

You might say that Stanley is thrown out of adjustment in scene 2, when Stella says, "we've—lost Belle Reve!" and argue that his objective is to find out why, since under the Napoleonic Code he owns half the property. But is that arc of action Stanley's through-line? Nothing is made of his property rights after scene 2.

In the interpretation that has Blanche as the leading character, her arc of action covers the entire play. She is thrown out of adjustment prior to the play's opening, and the climax starts toward the end of scene 11, the final scene in the play, where she tries to run. There remains, then, only a brief resolution—her adjusting to the loss of her struggle and deciding to go with the Doctor.

You may say that making Blanche the leading character violates the criteria of the leading character being volitional, and you might argue that in scene 11 she is incapable of making a rational choice. But is Blanche clinically insane? Reality and illusion are major subjects in Williams' writing, and he always sides with the person for whom illusion is a necessity. In *Portrait of a Madonna*, the Elevator Boy says of Miss Collins (a forerunner of Blanche), "I didn't know that she'd been nuts *that* long," and the Porter replies:

> Who's nuts an' who ain't? If you ask me the world is populated with people that's just as peculiar as she is.... There's important people in Europe got less'n she's got. Tonight they're takin' her off 'n' lockin' her up. They'd do a lot better to leave 'er go an' lock up some of them maniacs over there. She's harmless, they ain't. They kill millions of people an' go scot free!

It might be argued that, to a degree, Blanche is actually volitional at the play's end. Note how Williams describes the Doctor and Matron: "The gravity of their profession is exaggerated—the unmistakable aura of the state institution with its cynical detachment," and later, "divested of all the softer properties of womanhood, the Matron is a peculiarly sinister figure in her severe dress. Her voice is bold and toneless as a firebell." Blanche's response to these characters, then, is far from irrational.

True, the expressionistic devices, the "lurid reflections", the sound of the "Varsouviana,"" the echo chamber's cries and noises of the jungle" are obviously from Blanche's mind, but do they not show her understandable panic and fear of the situation rather than clinical insanity?

After making a decision to go with the Doctor, it might be argued that this is a deliberate choice that further reveals Blanche's character. When Stella cries out her name, and as she walks on without turning, perhaps Blanche is making a deliberate *act of kindness*, since she knows her sister must go on living with Stanley. She may also detect the Doctor's Southern-gentleman manners and believe she has a chance—through manipulation—of surviving in a mental institution.

> MATRON: These fingernails have to be trimmed. (The Doctor comes into the room and she looks at him.) Jacket, Doctor?
>
> DOCTOR: Not unless necessary. (He takes off his hat and now he becomes personalized. The unhuman quality goes. His voice is gentle and reassuring as he crosses to Blanche and crouches in front of her. As he speaks her name, her terror subsides a little. The lurid reflections fade from the walls, the inhuman cries and noises die out and her own hoarse crying is calmed.) Miss DuBois. (She turns her face to him and stares at him with desperate pleading. He smiles; then he speaks to the Matron.) It won't be necessary.
>
> BLANCHE: (faintly) Ask her to let go of me.
>
> DOCTOR: (to the Matron) Let go. (The Matron releases. Blanche extends her hands toward the Doctor. He draws her up gently and supports her with his arm and leads her through the portières.)
>
> BLANCHE: (holding tight to his arm) Whoever you are—I have always depended on the kindness of strangers.

You may think that Blanche surely is demented to believe she can find a "cleft in the rock of the world" in a state mental institution in the mid-1940s in Louisiana. But might it be argued that most of the sensitive, un-alikes and artists, *do* depend on the kindness of strangers? They *do* constantly hope and they *do* not want realism, they want "magic!" Certainly Blanche's struggles to remain free from restraint in scene 11, after she realizes that the Doctor is not Shep Huntleigh, is the highest point of action in the play, and it is still within the confines of the leading character's arc of action.

Further, it is evident that Williams has given much more background information about Blanche than Stanley. Why? Because Williams wants us to understand this enormously complex character. She needs full development since she is the only possible character who can arouse the requisite "pity and terror" of catharsis that a tragedy demands of its audience.

As to character, as discerned via choices and actions, Stanley's major decision whether to defend his lair or "get back" are unattractive, primitive, and simplistic choices. To give Blanche the bus ticket is cruel, but it is nothing compared with raping her when she is drunk and almost beside herself with anxiety. Does leveling her sexually, as he did her sister ("You showed me the snapshot of the place with the columns. I pulled you down off them columns and how you loved it, having them colored lights going!") reveal Stanley as a "good" person?

Even with the rampant male chauvinism of the 1940s, it seems improbable that Williams's intent was for an audience to feel compassion for Stanley rather than Blanche. This is not to say that Stanley is "all bad" and that Blanche is "all good." Certainly, the actor who plays Stanley will have to find the "good" in his character.

Blanche has more "bad" qualities than many leading characters. The farthest extreme an author could possibly go would be to make a character 49% "bad" and 51% "good." Blanche hovers near the dangerous edge of this extreme—dangerous because if she is too "bad," an audience may not be able to empathize with her. But everything in the play, from her first entrance ("There is something about her uncertain manner, as well as her white clothes, that suggests a moth") to her heroic physical struggle for freedom at the end, is calculated to bring out the viewer's understanding, sympathy, and empathy.

Finally, a production with Blanche as the leading character is far more harmonious with Williams's life view. Note what Williams wrote in the introduction to his collection of one-act plays, *27 Wagons Full of Cotton*:

> The biologist will tell you that progress is the result of mutations. Mutations are another word for freaks. For God's sake let's have a little more freakish behavior—not less. Maybe 90 per cent of the freaks will be just freaks, ludicrous and pathetic and getting nowhere but into trouble. Eliminate them however—bully them into conformity—and nobody in America will be really young any more and we'll be left standing in the dead center of nowhere.[6]

To whom in *A Streetcar Named Desire* do the words "freakish," "ludicrous," and "pathetic" better apply—Stanley or Blanche?

Of the play itself, Williams said that it is a vision of "anthropological regression," and that "the apes will inherit the earth."[7] This theme implies that the apes should *not* be allowed to take over; that there should be humane compassion and tolerance for those who are more sensitive and less able to cope. Blanche's life goes from hope to resignation. Why? Because the sensitive are overrun by the apes.

The point of this discussion is not to prove that only one interpretation for *A Streetcar Named Desire* exists. The analysis above could—and should—be challenged and debated. All practitioners should filter their understanding of a story's theme through the prism of their own life experience, which guarantees that no two people will view the same drama exactly the same way. But this does nothing to refute the proposition that a theme exists in the play that can only be discovered through an analysis of the relationship to one's own experience.

Ambiguities

We have so far focused on themes expressing the idea that life changes and offering to explain why such change occurs. But not all drama does

FAULKNER'S NOBEL PRIZE SPEECH

I believe that man will not merely endure; he will prevail. He is immortal, not because he alone among creatures has an inexhaustible voice, but because he has a soul, a spirit capable of compassion and sacrifice and endurance. The poet's, the writer's, duty is to write about these things. It is his privilege to help man endure by lifting his heart, by reminding him of the courage and honor and hope and pride and compassion and pity and sacrifice which have been the glory of his past. The poet's voice need not merely be the record of man, it can be one of the props, the pillars to help him endure and prevail.

"Faulkner's Nobel Speech, Literature, 1949," ed. Horst Frenz (Amsterdam: Elsevier Publishing Company, 1969). You can find the entire speech on the Internet.

this. A few years after the end of the Second World War, in the industrialized West, a view of life arose that rejected this notion.

Unlike William Faulkner, whose Nobel Prize acceptance speech represents a former era's literary Zeitgeist, some post-Second World War writers felt the idea that people could effect meaningful change was a cruel delusion. Humankind seemed caught in the grasp of impersonal forces against which struggle appeared fruitless. The catastrophic events of the twentieth century—the two world wars, the depression, the threat of nuclear annihilation, the alienation and isolation of modern life—seemed to reduce the individual to a state of utter powerlessness. A drama emerged whose themes reflected this point of view, often referred to as the *Theater of the Absurd*, a term coined by the critic Martin Esslin.

Earlier, we mentioned the cyclical form and noted that it does not incorporate the architectural components and especially the structural parts of plot found in more traditional forms of drama. For example, in *Waiting for Godot*, the absence of a clear beginning, a recognizable crisis decision, and a climax that produces a substantial change of the fortunes of the characters separate it from, say, *Macbeth* or *Jaws*.

This is no accident or ignorant oversight on the part of the author. On the contrary, it is entirely intentional. Structural parts of plot in *Macbeth* or

Jaws are inseparably connected to the idea that life goes through important changes over the course of the drama. The theme of a play like *Waiting for Godot*, however, is just the opposite: life does *not* change, and all our attempts to effect a transformation are ultimately futile and absurd. No matter what Vladimir and Estragon do, they are destined to end up on the same country lane, by the same solitary tree, playing the same distracting games to no discernible effect. In other words, the circular form of the play's structure is in complete harmony with its theme. Any attempt to suddenly append a climax that would produce meaningful change would completely undermine the point of view of the author.

The same forces that produced the circular plot also generated points of view about existence that strongly deviated from tradition. What were once considered the operating factors of human existence—morality, ethics, religious beliefs, even language itself—were seen as relative rather than absolute, open to a wide variety of interpretations and meanings. Life appeared less certain, less clear, and some drama reflected this shift in perception through themes that were ambiguous or, to some observers, impenetrable, intentionally obtuse, hard to define, or even hard to identify. A play or film might seem to be about *something*, but what, exactly?

COWARD ON *GODOT*

I have just read, very carefully, *Waiting for Godot* and in my considered opinion it is pretentious gibberish, without any claim to importance whatsoever. I know that it received great critical acclaim and I also know that it's silly to go on saying how stupid the critics are, but this really enrages me. It is nothing but phoney surrealism with occasional references to Christ and mankind. It has no form, no basic philosophy and absolutely no lucidity. It's too conscious to be written off as mad. It's just a waste of everybody's time and it made me ashamed to think that such balls could be taken seriously for a moment.

Noel Coward, *The Noel Coward Diaries*, ed. Graham Payn and Sheridan Morley (Boston, Toronto: Little Brown and Co., 1982), 444–445.

The theme of *Waiting for Godot*, for example, has confused—and frustrated—more people than have claimed to understand it. In 1960, Noel Coward gave his opinion of the play, and one can understand his response. His own work, rooted in more traditional structures of dramatic storytelling, had very little in common with the absurdist theme and form of *Waiting for Godot*. Moreover, he had been vilified by the critics after World War II as a writer of superficial diversions, only to be rediscovered and knighted in the mid-1960s. That a play that seemed so willfully to defy tradition and rational interpretation should be embraced, while his own work suffered a reversal in reputation, probably rankled.

And he was certainly not alone. *Godot* has been called a "drama of non-communication," "a death rattle brought to the stage" and "a humorous lament for the failure of the finite self to make contact with the Other, the witness that is outside space and time."[8] As if these descriptions weren't ambiguous enough, Becket himself, speaking of his writing, said the most important word was "perhaps."[9]

Yet the play persists. Is it possible to conclude that the theme of the play—whatever it is—clearly resonates with some audiences? The ambiguity of its meaning must, on some level, mirror the ambiguity people see in a life once ruled by comforting sureties.

And it should be noted that not everyone has found the play all that ambiguous. *Godot* was staged at San Quentin prison in 1957. Unlike other, more sophisticated audiences, the inmates were said to have no trouble identifying with the play and, according to reports, they watched with rapt attention. The futility of change and the uncertainty of human existence seemed to make perfect, immediate sense to men serving sentences in a maximum-security prison.[10]

Universality

A Raisin in the Sun is about Walter Lee Younger, an African American living in a specific era in American history. We see him, however, as typical of all men and women whose dreams have been deferred. We view Nora's struggle in *A Doll's House* not just in terms of a specific woman's struggle in

Norway in the 1880s, but also in terms of the struggle we all go through to obtain our individuality and independence.

In *Ghosts*, Ibsen was so concerned with universalizing his theme that he refused to leave it to the imagination of the audience. Mrs. Alving says, "I am timid and faint-hearted because of the ghosts that hang about me [that] I can never quite shake off." Then Ibsen goes from the specific to the general: "I sometimes think we are all ghosts.... It is not only what we have inherited from our father and mother that 'walks' in us. It is all sorts of dead ideas, and lifeless old beliefs ... they have no vitality, but they cling to us all the same." Then he takes yet another step toward the universal: "Whenever I pick up a newspaper, I seem to see ghosts gliding between the lines. There must be ghosts all the country over, as thick as the sands of the sea. And then we are, one and all, so pitifully afraid of the light."

There is a tendency of modern makers of drama to be a little bit less "on the money"; to express the theme of their work more circumspectly than Ibsen does in *Ghosts*. The goal of many contemporary dramatic artists—Harold Pinter comes to mind—is to urge members of the audience to sort through the intended ambiguities and come to their own conclusions regarding the drama's theme.

But the drive to universalize experience is no less important in holding an audience's attention now than it was in 1881. What explains the popularity of Tony Kushner's *Angels in America*? The play is subtitled *A Gay Fantasia on National Themes*—themes being used to mean subject matters or subjects. Most of its leading characters are gay. Yet the play is clearly about more than being homosexual. It touches on universal subjects such as love, death, loyalty, power, sexuality, and bigotry, and suggests that dishonesty in these matters leads to self-destruction and that it is better to confront our fears than to run from them. Being gay, then, is no more a prerequisite in relating to this theme than being Danish is necessary for a full appreciation of *Hamlet*.

Or is it?

Artists have often had to negotiate the difficult path between making a living and holding on to their vision and values. It would be interesting to see what would happen if *Angels in America* were presented to an audience intolerant of homosexuality. There would undoubtedly be—and in fact has been—much opposition, not only to the theme, but its means of development.

When Frau Hedwig Niemann-Raabe, a leading German actress who was a big box-office draw, demanded Ibsen write a "conciliatory" ending for her production of *A Doll's House*, Ibsen accommodated this "barbaric outrage" by writing the following:[11]

NORA: ... Goodbye. (Going)

HELMER: Go then! (seizing her arm) But first you shall see your children for the last time!

NORA: Let me go! I will not see them! I cannot!

HELMER: (Drawing her over to the door) You shall see them (opening the door, speaking softly) Look, there they are asleep, peaceful and carefree. Tomorrow, when they wake up and call for their mother, they will be—motherless.

NORA: (trembling) Motherless ...

HELMER: As you once were.

NORA: Motherless! (struggling with herself, letting her traveling bag fall.) Oh, this is a sin against myself, but I cannot leave them. (half sinking down by the door)

HELMER: (joyfully, but softly) Nora! (The curtain falls.)[12]

Ibsen clearly did not want to alter the theme of his play in this way, but felt compelled to do so for practical considerations. The actress was a star, a star means an audience, and without an audience there can be no financial success. But note the subtlety of this rewritten ending: Ibsen's insistence on Nora's line—"Oh, this is a sin against myself"—which, even in her capitulation, the play seems to be saying that, although a woman's first duty is toward her family, Nora is not being true to herself.

As with Ibsen, Tennessee Williams also had to face compromise but his was a double whammy. In director Kazan's Broadway Production as Blanche makes her final exit, Stanley kneels beside Stella and putting his fingers into the opening of her blouse says, "(voluptuously, soothingly), Now, honey, Now, love. Now, now, love" and Stella's "luxurious sobbing" succumbs to a "sensual murmur." This ending seems to reinforce the topic of anthropological regression by indicating that the apes will inherit the earth.

In the film version under the watchful eye of both the Hollywood Production Code as well as the Catholic Legion of Decency, Stella runs upstairs to Eunice's apartment saying she will never go back to Stanley. Although, this ending reinforces the side of William's point of view that brutes should not be allowed to inherit the earth, paradoxically, the action reads as contrived and uncharacteristic of both Stanley and Stella—a quick fix—since it does not include an equal measure of the theme's view that although the brutes should not be allowed to win, they very often do.

To summarize: Theme, in this context, does not refer to the subject matter of a drama. It concerns the artist's point of view on the subject matter. It often deals with the possibility of change in human existence and what accounts for that change if it occurs. In the second half of the twentieth century, writers have been drawn to themes of a more ambiguous nature than has historically been the case, which reflects shifting attitudes toward the nature of human experience. Whatever the theme, and however clearly or obscurely it is demonstrated, all architectural components of the drama should unite to reflect it in one way or another.

Notes

1. Aristotle, *The Poetics of Aristotle*, trans. Preston H. Epps (Chapel Hill: University of North Carolina Press, 1942), 24.

2. Robert McKee, *Story: Substance, Structure, Style and Principles of Screenwriting* (London: Methuen Publishing, Ltd., 1999), 118.

3. Tennessee Williams, *27 Wagons Full of Cotton and Other Plays* (New York: New Directions, 1966), x.

4. Aristotle, *Poetics*, 17.

5. Aristotle, *Poetics*, 24.

6. Williams, *27 Wagons Full of Cotton*, xii.

7. Tennessee Williams, "The Angel of the Odd," *Time* (9 March 1962): 53.

8. Michael Robinson, *The Long Sonata of the Dead: A Study of Samuel Beckett* (New York: Grove Press, 1969), 231; Farris Anderson, *Alfonso Sastre* (New York: Twayne Publishers, Inc., 1971), 69; and Ronald Hayman, *Samuel Beckett* (New York: Frederick Ungar Publishing, Co., 1973), 28.

9. Tom Diver, "Beckett by the Madeleine," an interview at the Columbia University Forum IV (Summer 1961), 23.

10. Martin Esslin, *The Theatre of the Absurd* (New York: Anchor Books, Doubleday and Co., 1961), xvii.

11. Henrick Ibsen, *A Doll's House*, trans. James Walter McFarlane (London: Oxford University Press, 1961), 87–88.

12. Ibsen, *A Doll's House*, 87–88.

Genre

You've been through it a thousand times. You and your friend are looking through the paper, trying to decide what movie to see. You scan the ads, maybe read a thumbnail review or two, or try to recall a friend's comments on a new release. Choices are made and rejected. You can't seem to agree, and the hands of the clock are moving. Soon, one of you must compromise or it's Scrabble and television for the rest of the evening. Sound familiar? You may not know it, but you are arguing over *genre*, the fourth architectural component of production in our discussion.

In a situation like this, what is the bone of contention? The actors in the movie? The location of the theater? The length of the film? Whether it's in French (with subtitles) or English? The costume design? The director? Probably none of the above. Usually, the disagreement is over the *kind* of movie you want to see. You're in the mood for a romantic comedy, but your friend wants to see a sci-fi film.

Dramatic literature can be divided and categorized into distinct genres. In *Poetics*, Aristotle separated drama into two fundamental genres: tragedy and comedy. Eighteen hundred years later, in Shakespeare's *Hamlet*, we have the following scene between Polonius and Hamlet.

> POLONIUS: The actors are come hither, my lord.
>
> HAMLET: Buz, buz!
>
> POLONIUS: Upon my honour,—
>
> HAMLET: Then come each actor on his ass,—
>
> POLONIUS: The best actors in the world, either for tragedy, comedy, history, pastoral, pastoral-comical, historical-pastoral, tragical-historical, tragical-comical-historical-pastoral, scenes individable, or poems unlimited.

The number of categories has increased. Robert McKee exceeds Polonius' eight by roughly sixty genres and subgenres, everything from redemption plots to prison drama to disaster/survival stories.[1] And how about Netflix? You will find twenty major categories from Action & Adventure to Television. There are 440 sub and sub-sub headings, focusing on such categories as fiction, documentary, age, country, and so forth.

So, news? No, we know you already know this. All of the above deals with matters of commerce, which is post-production and not the focus of our book. What the above does, however, is serve to keep us on the same page.

Although we will be discussing genre "conventions," which deal with dramatic devices, characters, and subject matter that audiences have come to associate with a particular genre, this is not our focus. Anyone interested in the conventions can go to a bookstore's film and TV section and find a cottage industry of how-to manuals guaranteeing fame and fortune if the future writer hews to all the tricks of the conventions.

Our focus is on *desired audience response* and how this affects character-dimension and density of plot in the five basic genres—tragedy, drama, melodrama, comedy, and farce—and their history and mutation throughout the 2,500 years of Western thought and civilization.

Returning to the example of the couple who can't agree on what flick to see, what accounts for the disagreement? When someone says, "I don't feel like a romantic comedy tonight," she's saying she knows full well what response that genre produces, and she's not in the mood. In fact, so sure are we of the relationship between genre and response that the mere mention of the genre can be enough to persuade or dissuade us from renting a film.

The young man in our introduction who wants to tell his story about dying to dance the tango with the beautiful woman in red knows from the very second he begins how he would like his listeners to respond: whether to laugh at his folly or pity his humiliation. He does not think about genre. He doesn't have to; he just naturally wants his audience to take his story in a certain way. This is what practitioners need to ferret out before and during the production: what is the creator's intention as to audience reaction?

Elia Kazan quotes Thornton Wilder, warning him against mixing styles (actually, he means genres). He blamed it on what he felt was his less-than-successful film, *A Face in the Crowd*. The first part was satirical, inviting laughter from the viewer at the bumbling hick character, Lonesome Rhodes. In the second part, the genre changed to drama, requiring the audience to become sympathetic and emotionally involved with the character.

Kazan says that at the beginning of any dramatic story, a contract is made with the audience as to how they are to react to the plot and characters. Once that contract is made and carried out, it is very difficult for viewers to shift to another. Kazan concluded that, in the beginning, "If I had made [the leading character] more humanly attractive, it might have been less funny, but it could have made the two parts coherent."[2]

It is true that the mixing of genres is one of the reasons why dramatic storytelling fails, but there is another side to this story. In the case of Chekhov, a lack of understanding of the author's intent may have done much to make him successful. Chekhov saw *The Cherry Orchard* as comedy, while Stanislavsky, the director, saw it as tragedy—genres that ask for a diametrically opposite response from their audiences. "Ironically enough, despite Chekhov's conviction of the Art Theatre's misinterpretation of *Orchard*, it became the most successful of all his plays and was retained in their repertoire for years."[3] Go figure!

It should be noted that Kazan's admonition doesn't apply to every play or period. Shakespeare was surely not trying to alienate his audience by juxtaposing the broad comedy of the gravedigger scene with the tragedy of Hamlet's impending death. But he didn't do it out of ignorance or disregard. Such a contrast between the comic and tragic was not at odds with the truth of life as Elizabethans saw it. For them, tragedy and comedy could exist in the same emotional space—if not in the same scene, then certainly in the same play.

For the Greeks or Romans, however, such apposition would have been unthinkable, except when tragedy was being burlesqued in the satyr plays. The French and Italian Neoclassicists were even more explicit in their injunctions. Woe to the playwright who went afoul of the strict rules governing genre laid down by the powerful French Academy in the 1630s. Yet today, genres are mixed and matched in ever increasing and inventive ways. It is almost impossible to see a Hollywood film in the crime genre that doesn't include a healthy dose of irony. Ironic comedy has become so central to the modern American ethos that even when dealing with kidnaping and murder—as in the film *Fargo*—there is an undercurrent of amused detachment. We are meant to be revolted *and* to laugh at a chainsaw dissection of a corpse, to want the criminals to come a cropper, while taking delight in their idiosyncrasies.

To compare modern versions of the crime genre with those from the 1930s and 1940s, with their serious comportment and moral clarity, is to see just how cynical and jaded American culture has become in the intervening years, and how the expected response from a particular genre has evolved and mutated as a result of that change.

We are an age deeply suspicious of those in power and much more attuned to the possibilities, indeed, the probabilities of abuse and corruption. It is said that in the mid 1950s, American public opinion polls frequently listed the president and heads of corporations as the most respected and trusted figures in the land. Polls taken today do not offer a similar view toward those sitting comfortably atop the political and corporate power structure.

This attitude reflects a growing skepticism toward traditional notions of who is good and who is bad. *The Godfather* transformed the traditional figure of the Mafioso boss into a loving and devoted family man trying to do what is best for his family. Rather than dying at the hands of an avenging criminal justice system, he suffers a heart attack while chasing his beloved grandson around the garden of his luxurious estate. Moreover, his death is calculated to produce sadness rather than approbation. Such a reaction would not have been possible for an audience until the culture was morally configured to allow for such a representation.

The evolution of the crime genre not only reforms and romanticizes the criminal but often demonizes law enforcement and traditionally respectable civic leaders of one kind or another. In *The Godfather*, there is not a single representative of these professions who is not portrayed as a detestable hypocrite. A police captain is in the pay of a rival mob family; a senator is found in bed with a murdered prostitute; American business leaders hobnob with the corrupt dictator of Cuba.

More to the point, we now accept these depictions as truthful. When Don Corleone confesses to his son, Michael, that his dream was that someday he would become a judge or a politician, we may not be thrilled with the prospect, but we do not mutter, "That's impossible, someone unscrupulous becoming a judge or politician!"

Compare *The Godfather* with the great crime stories of the 1930s and 1940s: *Little Caesar, The Public Enemy, The Petrified Forest, Double Indemnity, Notorious, Key Largo, White Heat,* and scores of others. They all share the same view—moral clarity, nay *certainty*—toward crime: you can never get away with it. There are, of course, still crime dramas that express this view. An example is *Excellent Cadavers,* a docudrama (1999) about Italian lawmakers fighting the Mafia, in which the criminals are actually vanquished by the forces of justice. Not every example of the modern crime drama, it would seem, has turned the underworld gang into the Walton family.

Let's take a closer look at the five genres to which we referred at the beginning of the chapter, starting with the granddaddy of them all ...

Tragedy

Not surprisingly, the first person to render a detailed examination of genre was Aristotle. Indeed, his *Poetics* in large part deals with the specific effect tragedy is intended to have upon an audience. While not everyone today agrees with the entirety of Aristotle's analysis, his writing is so insightful that it bears in-depth discussion.

In common usage today, the word "tragic" tends to mean any devastating or pitiable event. A busload of children die in an accident, an elderly grandmother is hit by a motorcycle as she crosses the street, a teenager dies of leukemia, and all these events are called "tragedies." The effect produced on the observer is extreme sadness and loss, combined with a sense that the event shouldn't have happened.

Aristotle, however, was onto something far more comprehensive and penetrating. Analyzing the Greek drama that he both read and saw, he defined tragedy as:

> an imitation, through action rather than narration, of a serious, complete, and ample action, by means of language rendered pleasant at different places in the constituent parts by each of the aids [used to make language more delightful], in which imitation there is also effected through pity and fear its catharsis of these and similar emotions.[4]

Only one part of the above definition applies solely to the tragic genre. "Imitation through action, rather than narration" applies to all genres. The genres drama and melodrama are "serious." The vast majority of dramatic stories are "complete" (meaning they have a beginning, middle, and end) and "ample" (meaning they have a proper magnitude), and all use language for the purpose of communication (although not all use pleasant and delightful language).

It is only the last part of the definition—"in which imitation there is also effected through pity and fear its catharsis of these and similar emotions"—that alone determines whether or not the work is a tragedy. The emotions of pity and fear are readily understandable. To pity is to feel sorry for, and to fear is to be afraid of. In Aristotle's view, we pity the leading character in tragedy because he does not deserve his fate, and we fear for him because we recognize his tragic fall could be our own.

In complete ignorance and as a result of the machinations of others, Oedipus committed the twin sins of killing his father and marrying his mother. In what sense, then, does he deserve his fate? He is traditionally described as "arrogant" and "over-prideful," which may indeed be true. But do those character traits, in and of themselves, justify what happens to him? Do we detect the workings of poetic justice in his fall? Do we say to ourselves, "Well, he surely had that coming?" We do not, or we would feel no pity.

The definition of catharsis is difficult to wrap one's head around. The dictionary gives several definitions, one of which—"evacuation of the bow-

CATHARSIS

On catharsis: No word used by Aristotle has caused more debate than this one, and readers will find many translations and explanations of it. One should begin ones reading in explanation of it with Bywater's lengthy note, and then read in other commentaries. Some notion of the controversy precipitated by the use of this word in this definition may be gained by consulting a University of North Carolina Master's dissertation.

* * *

Robertson's dissertation reveals that there are over *ninety* different interpretations, and concluded: It may be observed that the word catharsis as applied to aesthetics has no definitive meaning. Its denotations, as well as its connotations, vary considerably among persons who accept different interpretations. The variety of markedly different interpretations set forth by contemporary authorities, and the complex nature of these interpretations, make it impossible to use the word meaningfully without some sort of elaboration.

Robertson goes on to say that in view of this situation, unless one specifies exactly whose interpretation of catharsis he approves of, or explains at length exactly what he means by the term, his use of it can convey no more than a very amorphous signification to his listeners or readers.

Aristotle, *Poetics*, 11n2; and Durant Waite Robertson Jr., *A Preliminary Survey of the Controversy over Aristotle's Doctrine of Tragic Catharsis*, M.A. diss. (Chapel Hill: The University of North Carolina, 1937), 195–196.

---

els brought about by laxatives"—it seems safe to say, is *not* the meaning Aristotle had in mind. We believe that a relevant definition based on the word's Latin origin (*purgare*, or to purify), is the purifying of the spectator's emotions—pity and fear—gained through their empathic participation in the performance.

In doing so, there is indeed an evacuation of tensions that has coalesced and clogged the spectator's emotions. And this pattern of purgation found in classical tragedy is still clearly visible in later dramas, regardless of the evolutionary changes in society. Audiences who experience tragedy still feel an unexplainable and mysterious "high"—a kind of exaltation—as if they had achieved an understanding of the rightness of a universal order that surpasses individual fate.

Having arrived at the genre's intended response, Aristotle goes on to discuss the interdependent relationship between plot and character on the one hand, and the audience response on the other. He examines four different types of plot situations and character types, and as we have said before, anointed one as the ideal candidate: "The situation of a man of much glory and good fortune who is not [too] superior in excellence and uprightness and yet does not come into his misfortune because of baseness and rascality but through some inadequacy or positive fault." This last requirement being most commonly translated as "tragic flaw," is another way of saying that the tragic hero plays a role in his own downfall.

Here we have something that helps us distinguish between pathos—that which evokes pity or sadness—and tragedy as Aristotle envisaged it. If a small child obliviously wanders out into the street and is hit by a truck, such an event would be pathetic, but not tragic in the dramatic sense. A child cannot, in any meaningful sense, be regarded as the author of her own demise; her obliviousness to the danger of oncoming traffic is not a flaw in her character—an inadequacy or positive fault—but a characteristic of any child.

If, on the other hand, the father of the child, knowing full well the danger of leaving his child unattended, nevertheless, and in opposition to all his otherwise decent impulses, chooses to leave her on the corner to duck into a bar for a quick chat with a friend, and later emerges to see her struck down by a truck, then we have the makings of a tragic situation, since the father's fall into misfortune—not to mention the child's—was in large part the result of his own making.

Hamlet's fall, even as we acknowledge his role in it, seems to represent the workings of universal, timeless, and ultimately mysterious forces that no human being can ever fully comprehend. Whatever one calls these greater forces—fate, destiny, higher power—we take a certain pleasure in contemplating them, even—perhaps especially—if they lead to a tragic end. But what existential mystery is being examined by showing the random death of an innocent? That life is painful? Chaotic? Unfair? Old news! Or, to steal a line from Horatio, we need no ghost come from the grave to tell us that.

Perhaps the best way to illustrate both audience reaction and how plot and character enter into the tragic experience is to contrast two twentieth-century plays, also made into films, that are often referred to as tragedy: *A Streetcar Named Desire* and *Death of a Salesman.*

Both plays generate pity for their leading characters. Blanche DuBois is dislocated from the moment she walks on the stage in *Streetcar.* She brings with her a catalogue of painful memories from her past—self-destructive sexual encounters, family dysfunction, a husband dead from suicide caused perhaps by her remark on his homosexual encounter—and is both physically and psychologically brutalized by Stanley and Mitch over the course of the story. While she is not an entirely sympathetic character, we empathize with her for the multiple traumas from which she suffers even as we acknowledge the role she has played, and plays, in her own unhappiness.

Willy Loman, the leading character of *Death of a Salesman*, is a study in humiliation and alienation. Exhausted from a job he can no longer do, at odds with his sons, frustrated with what he sees as a failed life, haunted by comparisons to a successful older brother, he is a man fast approaching some sort of emotional disintegration. He, too, is not without flaws, yet like Blanche, he radiates a fragility that evokes our compassion and our pity.

If we pity Blanche because she does not deserve her misfortune, and if, in the moments of crisis and climax, we see ourselves in her, the terror we feel at her situation will nullify the pity that has been previously built throughout the play. We will, at the end, be totally drained of emotion and feel a strange kind of exhilaration, not only from our empathetic involvement, but also from the beauty of the play's perfect form, as well as from the safety of being distanced from actual happenings, since we are experiencing a play rather than real life. Audiences do not tend to cry at the end of *A Streetcar Named Desire.*

Contrast this with the effect produced by the crisis and climax of *Death of a Salesman*. First, Linda, and, then, Biff begin to suspect and fear Willy's intention to kill himself in a driving accident.

LINDA: (calling from within the house) Willy, are you coming up?

WILLY: (Uttering a gasp of fear, whirling about as if to quiet her.) Sh! (He turns around as if to find his way; sounds, faces, voices, seem to be swarming in upon him and he flicks at them, crying.) Sh! Sh! (Suddenly music, faint and high, stops him. It rises in intensity, almost to an unbearable scream. He goes up and down on his toes, and rushes off around the house.) Shhh!

LINDA: Willy?

(There is no answer. Linda waits. Biff gets up off his bed. He is still in his clothes. Happy sits up. Biff stands listening.)

LINDA: (With real fear) Willy, answer me! Willy!

(There is the sound of a car starting and moving away at full speed.)

LINDA: No!

BIFF: (Rushing down the stairs.) Pop!

(As the car speeds off, the music crashes down in a frenzy of sound, which becomes the soft pulsating of a single cello string.)

The fear is certainly Willy's, but even more so it is Linda and Biff's and the spectators', who know what he is going to do. Willy's fear of dying must be at its most acute just before he crashes his car, but this event occurs offstage. When the music transforms from a "frenzy of sound" to the "soft pulsating of the single string of a cello," this mournful sound contrasts the joyous sound of the flute used in the remembrance scenes, when leafy green trees branch high over the house, the family was young, the boys washed the Chevy, and Biff was a high school football star playing in the city championship game in Ebbets Field.

There is so much to like about Willy, especially his motives, and so little to dislike, other than his obsession with false material values and—on the road and lonely—his infidelity to Linda, that our pity is overwhelming at the conclusion of his arc of action. Added to this is the Requiem scene at the burial.

> LINDA: Why did you do it? I search and search and I search, and I can't understand it, Willy. I made the last payment on the house today. Today, dear. And there'll be nobody home. (A sob rises in her throat.) We're free and clear. (Sobbing more fully, released:) We're free. (Biff comes slowly toward her.) We're free ... We're free. (Biff lifts her to her feet and moves out up right with her in his arms. Linda sobs quietly. Bernard and Charley come together and follow them, followed by Happy. Only the music of the flute is left on the darkening stage as over the house the hard towers of the apartment building rise into sharp focus, and ... The Curtain Falls)

The scene leaves the audience with overwhelming pity, since the terror aroused in the audience during the crisis and climax is not sufficient to nullify it. In fact, far from being purged, we empathize more deeply with Linda, Biff, and Happy in the Requiem.

At the play's end, the audience at the original Broadway production was overwhelmed. The stunned silence, accompanied by muffled sounds of weeping, seemed to last and last before, finally, applause started with a single handclap and built ever so slowly to a crescendo during the curtain calls. And even after, when the house lights came up, the audience, rather than breaking into loud chatter and a rush to get a taxi as is typical of the Broadway crowd, left the theater slowly and quietly, as mourners after a funeral.

This does not seem to conform to the intended response Aristotle attributed to tragedy. What accounts for the difference of effect? A structural shift occurs in *Salesman* that does not appear in *Streetcar* in which Blanche is onstage for the entire crisis and climax. In *Salesman*, Willy literally leaves the stage to Linda, Biff, and Happy, along with us—the spectators— empathizing for and with them in their agonizing grief and thereby laying equal claim to Willy for our pity.

With Blanche, a demonic and self-destructive inner force is at work— *desire*—that she tries to combat or deny and can never deal with honestly because of her conditioned Southern gentility. Within the framework of her destiny, she participates in her own destruction. There are no such demons in Willy; there is only the system to blame—the capitalistic, competitive system that uses a man and then spits him out; the system that implants its false values of materialism in Willy and makes him a victim. As Miller said in his "Tragedy and the Common Man," the only "flaw" in Willy Loman is the "inherent unwillingness to remain passive in the face of what he conceives to be a challenge to his dignity, *his image of his rightful status*."[5] Only the passive, only those who accept their lot without active retaliation, are "flawless." In other words, in Miller's view, Willy Loman isn't truly flawed at all; on the contrary, it is those of us who submit without a fight to the system's degradations who are suffering from a fundamental error in judgment. It is hard to imagine Tennessee Williams taking a similarly blameless view of Blanche.

This is not to say that *Streetcar* is a better play than *Salesman*. Yet it is instructive to see how the conception and arrangement of the structural parts of the drama impact audience reaction.

The value of Aristotle's *Poetics* is not that it provides an unassailable, permanent, or universal basis for understanding the meaning of catharsis. It is that it establishes a model for understanding genre. This model— that the components of drama unite to produce a specific effect on the audience—has value independent of any set of conventions and meanings one attaches to particular definitions. In short, whatever the effect sought by the artist, the constituent parts of the drama should be arranged and interrelated in such a way as to achieve that effect.

Drama

The word drama is most often used generically to include not only all plays but also every aspect of theater practice. Denis Diderot (1713–1784), influenced by the English theater, especially Lillo's *The London Merchant, or The History of George Barnwell* (1731), is the one most responsible for codifying the criteria upon which the genre, *drama*, is classified.[6] At the time of his writing, traditional ideas about tragedy were being evaluated by scholars;

there were forerunners to drama in *le genre serieux*, bourgeois (i.e., middle-class) tragedy, sentimental comedy, and the plays "scornfully dubbed" *comedie larmoyante*" ("tearful comedy").[7]

By drama, Diderot meant a serious play, using prose rather than verse, which dealt with the "aspirations of the bourgeoisie."[8] It is in the critical dialogues published, along with his plays *Le Fils Naturel* (1757) and *Le Pere de la Famille* (1758), that he states how the new genre, *drame bourgeois*, would differ from tragedy.[9]

Drama would reflect, rather realistically, the milieu of the bourgeoisie: their vicissitudes, conflicts, and values.[10] Characters of various occupations were to be shown, and such occupations were to provide psychological motivation for the action. Family relationships were to be represented, revealing the importance of family ties.[11] Characters were individuals, not types. Acting style was to be less artificial, especially in the convention of direct address to the audience. Terrible situations were no longer hidden behind the scenes as in classical and neo-classical tragedy. Strong emotions were not suppressed.

The performance was to be made "real"—to have a certain verisimilitude—because "only through such reality could the play penetrate the hearts of men with the author's stern, direct and very simple morality."[12] Furthermore, reality was to be effected through a realistic stage setting ("fourth-wall convention") and acting, and the removal of the spectators from the stage.[13] "The events of *Le Fils Naturel* were taken from real life. The play was contemporaneous, the setting laid at Saint-Germain-en-Laye, twelve miles west of Paris, the time, 1757."[14]

There were "explicit stage directions," and Diderot "peppered his pages with exclamation points and broken-off sentences, in order to give some idea of the emphatic style of speech and the semi-inarticulateness of persons who labor under strong emotions."[15] Punctuation by the author was to help the actor interpret the intended emotions.

Diderot felt that the drama should express sentiments that were common to all people. "In France, the growth of sentiment, *la sensibilite*, had affected the general character of comedy, causing it to become less satirical than it had been with Moliere."[16] Diderot wanted "to make art more comprehensive, more tolerant, more universal," and not exclude "as vulgar, cheap, contemptible, emotions to which a large number of our fellow men are responsive. Let the stage no longer be aristocratic, but popular, so that its appeal may be wider."[17]

Finally, and most important as far as audience reaction is concerned, drama was to include a moral lesson. In act 4 of *Le Fils Naturel*, after Constance says, "only the bad man lives alone,"[18] there follows a scene regarding virtue, centered around Dorval's illegitimacy and the possibility of his "sin" being passed on to his children. The "principal object" of Diderot's writing *Le Fils Naturel* "was to make the theatre an institution for teaching morality."[19]

To this end, Diderot believed that it was not enough for plays to merely entertain, "They must also impel to virtuous action." In an ideal society, "actors would fulfill the function of preachers." What is the purpose of dramatic composition? Diderot replied, "I believe it is to inspire among men a love of virtue and a horror of vice."[20]

In its evolution—especially after the Industrial Revolution, Marx, and the rise of the proletariat—the purpose of drama would change from "teaching morality" to presenting social, psychological, and economic points of view. Thus it might be correct to say that tragedy shows a struggle against insurmountable odds, such as the gods or fate, in which there is effected a catharsis, while drama shows a struggle against manmade institutions, which can be changed if, in the presentation, the audience member is enlightened and inspired with a love of good and an abhorrence of evil. The former struggle would produce *Oedipus* and *King Lear*; the latter, *Ghosts* and *Death of a Salesman*.

Melodrama

Have you ever observed a person, being told a hard-luck story, placing an imaginary violin on his shoulder and humming "Hearts and Flowers?" This is a parody of melodrama, which was itself a further mutation of the genre drama.

The segue from Diderot's drama to melodrama was a logical transition. It differed in significant ways, especially in the inclusion of the proletariat as characters and its concentration on suspense to "hook" the viewer. It also included outdoor scenic elements such as mountains, gorges, and rivers, whereas dramas tended to be set in formal drawing rooms where people talked about what happened outside. Melodrama produced its share of pity and fear and other heightened emotions as well as addressing socially significant issues. But its uniqueness was in its use of music to announce entrances and exits and to enhance sentiment and violent physical actions.

In *Le Fils Naturel*, Diderot discussed the problem of fitting prosody to music.[21] All authorities on the genre melodrama suggest that the first— inasmuch as history is able to determine the first in anything—to do this was Jean Jacques Rousseau, who "used music in his one-act play *Pygmalion* (1770) to express the emotions of a character or situation as the actor first pantomimed them and then conveyed them in words."[22] This device of using music as background for action, especially sentimental or violent physical action, is still in use to this day.

Guilbert de Pixérécourt (1773–1844) popularized melodrama in the working-class theaters of Paris. Indeed, he was called "The Corneille of the Boulevard," contrasting the differences between melodrama and the more aloof, high-toned (and less entertaining) neoclassic tragedies of Corneille.

He was quoted as saying, "I write for those who cannot read,"[23] which tells us something about the essence of melodrama and its audience; clearly, a forerunner of much of what we see on television today.

The American actor and playwright, William Gillette, himself the author of the very successful melodrama *Secret Service* (1913), defined melodrama's essence:

> Melodrama is a form of dramatic composition in prose, partaking of the nature of tragedy, comedy, pantomime, and spectacle, and intended for a popular audience. Primarily concerned with situation and plot, it calls upon mimed action extensively and employs a more or less fixed complement of stock characters, the most important of which are a suffering heroine or hero, a persecuting villain, and a benevolent comic. It is conventionally moral and humanitarian in point of view and sentimental and optimistic in temper, concluding its fable happily with virtue rewarded, after many trials, and vices punished. Characteristically it offers elaborate scenic accessories and miscellaneous divertissements and introduces music freely, typically to underscore dramatic effect."[24]

There was an exaggerated sentimentality and a maximum of bourgeois morality—"Lips that touch liquor shall never touch mine!"—followed by a musical chord, *Ta Da!* A standard recognition scene might include a locket hung around the neck of a lost child. Action was provided by heroes tied to railroad tracks, heroines eschewing modesty and tearing off their red petticoats to flag down the train and save their man, and buzz-saws progressing inch by inch toward the hero tied to a table. And there was the inevitable happy ending for the good people and unhappy ending for the bad.

Melodrama was successful in producing suspense because, more than any other previous genre, its audiences could identify with and feel for the fate of the heroes. Historically, the more popular thrillers began to use eye-popping visual or eardrum-bursting special effects that eventually assumed an equal—indeed a codependent—role with plot in creating the desired suspense.

Uncle Tom's Cabin, a play based on Harriet Beecher Stowe's novel, one of the most popular American stage melodramas of the nineteenth century, contained an archetypal scene. Undergirded by breathtaking, suspenseful music, the runaway slave, Eliza, with her baby in her arms, is pursued on horseback by the villainous slave-trader Simon Legree. His baying bloodhounds, nipping at Eliza's heels, force her into a life-or-death crisis decision: she must traverse—barefooted—the churning ice floes of the Ohio River to escape to the North.

Apprehension and tension were heightened for the audience of *The Poor of New York* when an onstage, Lower East Side tenement building started burning, while Augustin Daly's *Under the Gaslight* included the heart-stopping spectacle of a man tied to a railroad track as the thundering engine of the train was heard approaching. The audience's insatiable appetite for vicarious chills and thrills produced by spectacular visual effects not only appeased but also spiked their addiction to suspense. This led to greater and greater effects, including floods, volcanoes, and Ben Hur in a chariot race in the Roman Coliseum.

Having helped create a new and greatly expanded audience, who were now accustomed to the belief that real things were happening to real people in real places, the theater's ability to provide all this was suddenly dwarfed by the invention of the motion-picture camera. Spectacle—least-honored of Aristotle's six constituent parts[25]—was now *de rigueur*, but the theater could no longer compete with the realistic images made by the motion-picture camera.

Where once the sight of orange- and red-colored china-silk streamers propelled upward by fans to simulate a tenement fire could thrill and chill, now a spectator could watch D. W. Griffith's 1916 melodrama, *Intolerance*, and see spectacularly realistic scenes of Belshazzar's feast in ancient Babylon and the 1572 Saint Bartholomew Massacre in Paris. These spectacles were intercut with a 1916 story in America of individuals attempting to save an innocent man from electrocution. As their car speeds toward the railroad crossing, a throbbing locomotive thunders toward it.

As for the distinctive use of music as background to enhance excitement and suspense, in his films, D.W. Griffith used bits and pieces from various composers and oversaw the creation of his own scores to accompany *The Birth of a Nation* and *Intolerance*. The music scores arrived at a theater along with the print of the film, and a piano player (often the local music teacher) would play it, viewing the film for various cues.

There was always background music for radio shows in the 1930s, and music accompanied most films as well as TV soap operas. Eventually, the Academy of Motion Picture Arts and Sciences gave an award for the best musical score.

The list of Hollywood melodramas that include visual spectacles and special effects has become endless to the point of cliché: killer sharks, extraterrestrials, sinking ocean liners, speeding buses, runaway meteors, locusts, not to mention snow, rain, hail, and other meteorological phenomenon. Equally enhanced through new technology are auditory spectacles that not only include the sounds of gunshots and explosions but also, in the case of the first installment of *Star Wars*, blowing an entire planet to smithereens.

Almost every film produced today by the American commercial film industry uses the melodramatic conventions we've discussed, particularly the use of a musical score, sometimes to the point where plot, character, and thought are treated as of secondary importance to the decibels provided by the sound technician, and music that sometimes seems to have nothing whatsoever to do with the film.

If the melodrama is working, audiences will literally be on the edge of their seats, bodies empathically reacting to the action. The hero is walking on the outer ledge of a building some twenty stories above the street, his hands gripping the jagged bricks above him when his foot slips on the icy ledge. What happens next? We'd tell you, but that would ruin the other staple convention of melodrama: the cliffhanger!

Comedy

Although the *Poetics* deals almost exclusively with tragedy, Aristotle has a great deal to say about comedy as well. The word *comedy* is mentioned twenty-seven times; comic is mentioned six times; malevolent satire, six; lampoon, two; humorous, one, and burlesque, one.

Aristotle said that comedy differs from tragedy inasmuch as it portrays men as "cheaper, more ordinary persons ... not entirely base, but are embodiments of that part of the ugly which excites laughter."[26] His etymological discussion concluded that "the word for comic actors [comodoi], is derived not from comadsein, meaning 'to revel,' but from the fact that these actors, being expelled from cities (comae) as unworthy of recognition, wandered from comae to comae [and thus came to be called comodoi]."[27]

He said the division of poetry into either tragedy or comedy caused the "inherent characters of the poets. The nobler poets portrayed noble deeds and deeds of noble individuals, while the cheaper ones portrayed deeds of cheap persons, writing malevolent satires at first, just as the nobler poets at first wrote hymns and encomia."[28] Up to the present time, comedy has not been considered as important as the genres of tragedy or drama. How many comedies have won the Academy, Tony, or Drama Critics' Awards or the Pulitzer?

Aristotle said, "both tragedy and comedy grew out of improvisations, tragedy eventuating from the improvisations of composer-leaders of dithyrambs and comedy from those of composer-leaders of phallic song rites."[29] In chapter 13 of Poetics, he indicates that "it is necessary, then, for the well arranged plot to be single rather than ... double in out-come."[30] Later he says of the double ending that it has two endings, one for the good and one for the bad characters, however, the pleasure this type of plot gives is inherent in comedy but foreign to tragedy: "for in comedy those who are enemies according to the plot—Orestes and Aegisthus, for instance—become friends at the end and go off stage without anyone's being killed by anybody."[31] In Ethics, he speaks of three comic character types: the pompous man, the mock-modest man, and the buffoon.[32] In chapter 5 of Poetics, he gives his definition of comedy:

> Comedy is, as we have said, an imitation of cheaper, more ordinary persons. They are not entirely base, but are embodiments of that part of the ugly which incites laughter. Now the part of the ugly which

excites laughter is that which has some flaw or ugliness which causes neither pain or harm, just as an ugly and distorted mask immediately brings laughter but causes no pain.... the early history of comedy is not known because comedy did not at first receive serious consideration. This is natural since early comedy was presented by volunteer actors, and it was not until later that the archon [appointed by the Athenian government to oversee the staging of plays at the City Dionysia] first granted a chorus to writers of comedy.[33]

Admittedly, this definition does not quite have the magisterial ring of his definition of tragedy given earlier. But critic Elder Olsen took care of that. He paraphrased Aristotle's definition of tragedy to make one for comedy: "Comedy is the imitation of a worthless action, complete and of a certain magnitude, in language with pleasing accessories differing from part to part, enacted, not narrated, effecting a katastasis of concern through the absurd."[34] He goes on to add:

Since this sounds very odd, I will explain it. By "worthless" or "valueless" action—the Greek word is *phaulos*—I mean one which is of no account, which comes to nothing, so that, on hindsight at least, it would seem foolish to be concerned about it. This is different from ending happily; the *Oresteia* of Aeschylus ends happily, but on hindsight you would never say that you were foolish to have taken the terrors of the House of Atreus seriously. Even the ordinary melodrama or adventure story involves things you are quite right to be concerned about, even though the hero escapes them all. But not comedy; you could call all comedy "Much Ado About Nothing."[35]

It is evident that the basis for the comedies of the great Athenian playwright, Aristophanes, was ridicule and the desired audience response was laughter at—rather than with—the person being ridiculed. This genre has been referred to as "old comedy" by generations of theater historians. It satirized political and public life, used a chorus, was openly licentious and abrasive, and employed somewhat individualized characters.

Of course, once you come up with a term like "old comedy," you also have to come up with "new comedy." Which is precisely what theater historians have done (there is also "middle comedy," too, but we will let that pass). New comedy is used to describe the plays of later Greek comic writers such as Menander. These plays focused on domestic situations, did not use a chorus, were not licentious or abrasive, and relied on stock characters. Sound familiar? That's right, new comedy is essentially the basis for just about every American television sitcom you have ever seen.

Farce

Perhaps farce should not be separated from comedy at all, since it is comedy with a greater degree of plotting and physical action. The genre's most important characteristic is that characters are typically obsessed with getting their objectives met. This is precisely where many of the action gags come from. The characters are so mono-focused on getting what they want, and the level of energy is so high, that they are constantly bursting through doors and falling over couches.

There are such farcical elements in most comedy, but when they predominate, the plotting is so dense there can be little development of character. Thus, stock types, easily recognized by the audience, are used. We don't need to develop the character of the snippy young maid, the henpecked husband, the dominating mother-in-law, etc. Audiences will instantly recognize them, for they exist in the Roman drama of Plautus through Molière and on into television.

Indeed, one could write a whole history of farce, starting with the Roman drama of Plautus, and moving to farces in the Medieval drama: in France, *La Farce de maître Pierre Pathelin* (c. 1440); in Germany, the Hans Sachs 1494–1576 farces; in England, *The Second Shepherd's Play* (c. 1500); and, later, the farces of John Heywood (c. 1479–c. 1580). Certainly, the Italian *commedia dell'arte* played improvised farces, and such companies influenced Moliere. Although recently there has been a tendency to think of his works as comedies of character, most are produced as farces.

One of the best modern farces is Brandon Thomas's *Charley's Aunt.* In 1892, Oxford undergraduates, Jack and Charley invite their girlfriends, Kitty and Amy for lunch with the intention of proposing. A fellow student, Fancourt, is showing off his costume for a student production in which he plays an old lady, when a telegram arrives saying that Charley's aunt will not be able to chaperone the luncheon. Fancourt is commandeered as a substitute and we know that Amy and Kitty would not for a moment, believe that dressed in his shabby Queen Victoria costume, he is a woman. But we quickly accept the "if"—IF they could be deceived, then this is what would happen and the play is off and running, the belly laughs roll in, as the deception is maintained.

The farces of Georges Feydeau have had a revival, especially *A Flea in Her Ear,* and there have been a number of farces on Broadway: *Noises Off, Lend Me a Tenor, Taking Steps,* and *Breaking Legs.* But in general, farce comedy is an endangered species, at least in American theater.

We concede that the hoped-for reaction from comedy can include every response from the loud, vigorous, appreciative laugh, known as the belly laugh, to simple smiling. However, it is unsatisfying to actors, not to mention difficult to judge the success of a comedy, if all the audience does is smile. Take the following scene between two actors, one young and the other a bit older, after they exit. Young Actor: (serious) "Did you think that scene went OK tonight?" Older Actor: "Are you kidding me? Of course. We wowed 'em! Didn't you hear 'em? They were smiling all the way to the back of the house."

We could go on to discuss satire, high comedy, dark comedy, and absurdist comedy, but the best way to understand any genre is for you to read plays or watch films that fall into those categories and decide for yourself what characteristics define and unite them.

The following is an excerpt from a letter written in 1960 by Joe Stockdale, co-author of this book, to a colleague seeking advice on directing a melodrama.

> The worse production I ever directed was *The Desperate Hours,* a melodrama by Joseph Hayes. The story is of three escaped convicts from

the federal prison in Terre Haute, Indiana, who hold a family hostage in Indianapolis. I read the novel from which the play was taken and got very involved in the character of the three gunmen. The actors who played these roles and I even went to the actual prison for background material.

I was very much concerned with psychological motivation. Rehearsals lasted six *long* weeks in which we probed all aspects of the psychopathic killers' characters. But a curious thing happened. As these characters became more "real," more fully developed, more complex, and more motivated, the play seemed less and less real. I began to see ways in which the family could escape; why did they not do so? And paradoxically, as the psychos became more real, all the other characters became less and less. Rehearsal became a nightmare until I finally figured it out.

The advice I am about to pass along sounds so cheap and unintellectual that I hesitate to do so, but.... If you are doing a *melodrama*, cast it to *type* and don't even think about characters. You only want *general* characteristics of the type; you are not looking for specifics, and don't start developing them. (Oh, how I hate to say this, but....) Emphasize the *actions*, with confidence that the audience will accept the play for *what it is*, and try not to make it *more* than it is. Just settle for an entertaining evening in the theatre in which you do your damndest to build tension in the audience and put 'em in a state of suspense and on the edge of their seats.

Do *not* rehearse too long, just long enough to learn the actions, the lines, and the rhythm of the beats and then a couple of days to polish. Above all, do not indulge in emotional recall, sub-text pauses, dredging up subjective motivation, and so forth. The key is that you and actors must agree to make the audience *believe* what is happening. If this is accomplished you will "hook" the audience and enjoy the run of the show (if it is not so long that you go brain dead). Play with a good tempo and rhythm, picking up cues, and play the various beats (character, objective, obstacle) for the clarity of form, building to a climax.

Another play which almost fooled me, but eventually did not, was *The Diary of Anne Frank*. There are, of course, lines such as "In spite of everything, I still believe that people are really good at heart," which hook you on theme, if you are predisposed that way, and there is a still greater trap in the background of anti-Semitism and the terrible threat of genocide. The Nazi atrocities at the various concentration camps for Jews and other "undesirables" of the third Reich are so hideous that you almost automatically think that *theme* and *subject matter* must be of the greatest importance and must be stressed. In other words, you start treating a melodrama as a *drama*.

But essentially, the response you want from an audience at a performance of this play is suspense; you want them to hope against hope that the eight people confined in this Amsterdam attic will somehow survive. It would, perhaps, be more appropriate, considering the Nazi/Jewish topic of this play if it were written as a tragedy, or drama. But the book was adapted by a couple of old time Hollywood pros, Frances Goodrich and Albert Hackett, and the major emphasis is on the creation of suspense: distant sirens, marching and running feet in the night, wondering if the cat will meow and give them away, Anne's nightmare cry, and so forth.

As an aside, it should be known that there is another dramatization of *Anne Frank* by Meyer Levin which is "privately published by the author for literary discussion." The Levin version is not a melodrama, as theme is stressed and the characters are three dimensional. Whether it is "better" than the official version, I have to leave to you to judge.

However, in the official version—the only one allowed by copyright law that can be produced—the characters are types, bordering almost on caricatures: the young girl, the young boy, the good mother, the good father, the selfish hysterical woman, etc. You must, of course, make these people credible *within their type*, but do not venture beyond their type or you will destroy the credibility of the plot.

Notes

1. Robert McKee, *Story: Substance, Structure, Style and Principles of Screenwriting* (London: Methuen Publishing, Ltd., 1999), 79–86.

2. Michael Ciment, *Kazan on Kazan* (New York: The Viking Press, 1974), 117–118.

3. Earnest J. Simmons, *Chekhov: A Biography* (Chicago: University of Chicago Press, 1962), 617.

4. Aristotle, *The Poetics of Aristotle*, trans. by Preston H. Epps (Chapel Hill: The University of North Carolina Press, 1942), 11.

5. Arthur Miller, "Tragedy and The Common Man," *Theatre Arts* (March 1949): 48.

6. Arthur M. Wilson, *Diderot, The Testing Years, 1713–1759* (New York: Oxford University Press, 1957), 269.

7. Robert Loyal Cru, *Diderot as a Disciple of English Thought* (New York: Columbia University Press, 1913), 298.

8. Wilson, *Diderot, The Testing Years*, 261.

9. Cru, *Diderot as a Disciple of English Thought*, 295.

10. Wilson, *Diderot, The Testing Years*, 269 and 281.

11. Wilson, *Diderot, The Testing Years*, 270.

12. Robert Loyal Cru, *Diderot as a Disciple of English Thought* [reprint] (New York: AMS Press, Inc., 1966), 326.

13. Wilson, *Diderot, The Testing Years*, 268.

14. Wilson, *Diderot, The Testing Years*, 269.

15. Wilson, *Diderot, The Testing Years*, 268.

16. Cru, *Diderot as a Disciple of English Thought* [reprint], 298.

17. Cru, *Diderot as a Disciple of English Thought*, 316.

18. Cru, *Diderot as a Disciple of English Thought*, 268–269.

19. Cru, *Diderot as a Disciple of English Thought*, 266.

20. Cru, *Diderot as a Disciple of English Thought*, 270.

21. Cru, *Diderot as a Disciple of English Thought*, 268–269.

22. *The Reader's Encyclopedia of World Drama*, ed. John Gassner and Edward Quinn (New York: Thomas Y. Cromwell Company, 1969), 661.

23. "As a refined connoisseur of the arts, a bibliophile and collector, an editor and annotator of books, it seems most unlikely that Pixerecourt ever said the words often attributed to him: 'I write for those who cannot read.' In fact, he tells us something quite different about his audience as readers in his essay on the new genre, 'Melodrama,' published in 1832" (quoted here from a Website on Guilbert de Pixerecourt, http://web.gc.cuny.edu/mestc/OtherPublications/PixerecourtIntro.htm).

24. Frank Rahill, *The World of Melodrama* (University Park: Pennsylvania State University Press, 1967), xiv.

25. Aristotle, *Poetics*, 15.

26. Aristotle, *Poetics*, 8–9.

27. Aristotle, *Poetics*, 5.

28. Aristotle, *Poetics*, 6.

29. Aristotle, *Poetics*, 7.

30. Aristotle, *Poetics*, 25.

31. Aristotle, *Poetics*, 26.

32. Aristotle, *Nicomachean Ethics*, trans., intro., and commentary by Sarah Broadie and Christopher Rowe (Oxford: Oxford University Press, 2002), Book 2, chap. 7, pp. 118–120.

33. Aristotle, *Poetics*, 8–9.

34. Elder Olsen, *The Theory of Comedy* (Bloomington: Indiana University Press, 1968), 46–47.

35. Olsen, *The Theory of Comedy*, 46–47.

Style

Oedipus, Hamlet, and *Death of a Salesman* are all written in different centuries, with different stories, different characters, and different structures. But what distinguishes them in style is the unique *mode, manner,* or *way* these works are created and presented. Our objective is to help practitioners and fans understand and interpret style as an aid that supports and enhances a film or theater production. After defining style and giving its historical periods, we will address it from the point of view of writers, architects, designers, directors, and actors, asking them a final question: are there actors who can still act the classics?

Although many people would be hard-pressed to give an exact definition of the word style, no one seems to have any problem using it in everyday conversation. A salesclerk holds up a gaudy Hawaiian shirt and the young buyer says, "Sorry, dude, not my style." Someone speaks of a public figure such as Jacqueline Kennedy Onassis hosting a state banquet with "great style." A teenage girl affectionately calls her girlfriend a "slut" because (a fad that may be history by the time you read this!) she considers it a cool "style" of address.

The word "style" is also used when commenting that a painting is in "the neo-impressionist style," meaning that it uses the distinctive and characteristic technique of pointillism (tiny dots of colors, which become blended in the viewer's eye) developed by Seurat.

The first three examples illustrate a vogue, or a prevailing fashion of a particular time. This is *not* the meaning of style that we are writing about. The fourth example illustrates an identification of a painting by comparing it with the distinctive or characteristic *way* in which Seurat expressed his view of reality. Although he may not have been the first to use the technique of pointillism, he was the one to popularize it, and the style has stood the test of time and influenced other painters. This *is* an example of what we will be talking about in this chapter.

Style addresses the unique manner in which something is made and used as well as how it is perceived. To analogize: Telephones are a particular kind of instrument defined by their function, which is communication. They might be either mounted on the wall or a desk, or they might be push-button, rotary, or cellular, which are all related to type (genre). However, wall phones might be made in the style of the Monarch wooden wall phone circa 1920, the antique pink payphone, or the Spirit of St. Louis wall phone. A desk phone might be made in the style of Southern Telecom porcelain retro, old-fashioned, 1920s candlestick, or the Eiffel Tower phone, differences which have nothing to do with the phone's function.

The word "style" is also used as a contrast to content. We criticize a pretentious play by saying, "There's less here than meets the eye." We speak of argument lacking in substance as being a triumph of style over content. In *Hamlet,* Gertrude famously begs Polonius for "more matter and less art," implying that his speech relies more on decorative language than meaningful insight.

Yet, for those of you who feel style is merely the outward wrap, the surface effect, and has nothing to do with perception, wrap your head around this: what would happen if the President of the United States, giving his annual State of the Union address to Congress, waltzed in wearing ripped jeans, a faded t-shirt, an iPod, sporting a purple mohawk and a nose ring? Would the congressional delegates and the audience simply shrug their shoulders and say, "Hmm, that's strange, never seen him dress like *that* before?" Very unlikely! In fact, this would be front-page news in every capital in the world. Why? After all, it's only clothing, hair, jewelry, and an MP3 player, right? Wrong! It isn't just those things, it's what those things represent, what they say about the person who wears or uses them, what that individual is expressing about himself.

Think again of the example of the telephone. Functionally, it doesn't matter whether it's a wall, desk, or cell phone, or whether it has a rotary dial or push buttons. You can still call someone on it. But now see yourself (use your imagination here) as a CEO, politically conservative, with an MBA from the Wharton School of Business, heading a gigantic corporation, thinking of merging with company X that has been in operation since 1900.

You enter X's lavish reception room and notice that all the phones are Monarch wooden wall circa 1920! You wonder whether the company tends to cling to antique practices? Or do they have a cash flow problem and can't afford an up-to-date system? Or they don't want to pay for a new system? You sit there staring in disbelief at those wall phones, thinking the company would probably cling to other antiquated practices; they must be cheap and oblivious to technological change.

You're outta there!

Now say you're a youngish CEO, a boomer with a BA from New Hampshire College. Sure, you toked a bit in your time, got thrown in the slammer in New York City when you were on a protest march against the bomb, and scuffled with the fuzz in front of the United Nations, but, hey man, hasn't everyone? You look around at the space and see the 1920s Monarch wall phones with a ring-the-operator gizmo on the right side. Wow! Maybe they have a live switchboard operator stashed in the building, like Lily Tomlin's Ernestine ("We don't care, we don't have to, we're the phone company!") from *Saturday Night Live*? You dig it! Nonconformists into retro technology! This CEO dude, who happens to be a woman, values tradition, is not a slave to fashion but cutting edge; she thinks outside the box and doesn't give a rat's butt what others are doing. She radiates confidence! Cool!

Your response: Bring it on! This deal is gonna be Synergy City!

Style in Historic Periods (the Isms)

Since style is a result of a consistent feeling toward experience, it is often classified in three different periods that reflect predominant and generalized modes: the classic, the romantic, and the realistic. We'll take on the classic period here with only a nod to the others. Books could be written about each of these periods, but by the time we finish a single "ism," you'll have the idea. Each period may include another—modes of feeling not being mutually exclusive—or there may be varying degrees of each mode in all three periods. They overlap, sometimes by hundreds of years. Rostand's *Cyrano de Bergerac*, written in 1897 during a high point in the realistic movement, takes place in the French Neoclassical period (1640–1655), but the prominent feeling of the work is romantic.

One might say that classicism was the prominent mode of expression from the fifth century B.C.E. up to the eighteenth century, the romantic mode existed from 1700 to about 1875, and the realistic mode from 1875 to about 1965. In the past few decades, we have been in a cultural revolution, which may be evolving into a new "ism" based upon a departure from our intellectual roots and values in Western thought and civilization into a strange combination—yin and yang—of Eastern spiritualism and materialism.

Classicism

In a 2006 op-ed piece in the *New York Times*, columnist David Brooks writes about Emilio Estevez's film, *Bobby*, describing the ugly manner in which J. Edgar Hoover informed Bobby Kennedy of President John F. Kennedy's assassination and the ensuing months of withering grief that devoured him. Bobby, notes Brooks, was wasting away, physically and emotionally. While on vacation, he read Edith Hamilton's *The Greek Way*, given to him by Jackie Kennedy. In Hamilton's seminal work on ancient Greek culture and thought, Bobby "found a world view that helped him explain and recover from the tragedy that had befallen him." Brooks notes that Bobby carried the book around with him for years thereafter, occasionally reading passages aloud in public. He underlined a particular passage that spoke to the optimism of the Greek citizen: "Life for him was an adventure, perilous indeed, but men are not made for safe havens. The fullness of life is the hazards of life. And, at the worst, there is that in us which can turn defeat into victory." Noting the effect on Kennedy, Brooks observed: "If there were doctors of the spirit, the Greeks' specialty was to take grief and turn it into resolution."[1]

Sure, Hamilton was gloriously pro Western thought and civilization, but there is no better way to understand the classic style than to read her book. This classical style denotes the principles and characteristics of Greek literature, architecture, and sculpture of the Periclean age (495–429 B.C.E.), or of any other whose principles and qualities are similar in spirit to those of the Golden Age of Greece. Those qualities are: formal elegance, simplicity, dignity, correctness, just and lucid conception, and order.

Greek literature "depended no more on ornament than the Greek statue." Edith Hamilton says: "It is plain ... direct, matter-of-fact ... when translated with any degree of literalness, bare, and so unlike what we are used to even to repel.... All the scholars who have essayed translations, have felt this informed difficulty and have tried to win an audience for what they loved and knew as so great by rewriting, not translating, when the Greek way seemed too different from the English."[2]

Miss Hamilton quotes the distinguished scholar, Professor Gilbert Murray: "I have often used a more elaborate diction than Euripides did because I found that, Greek being a very simple and austere language and English an ornate one, a direct translation produced an effect of baldness which was quite unlike the original."[3]

As for the style of architecture, if you were to describe the Parthenon of the Acropolis at Athens, built in the fifth century B.C.E., you might call it simple, formal, symmetrical, ordered (especially as it demonstrates a point of view in its relationship to land, sea, and sky—the whole to the parts or the parts to the whole), clean-lined, functional, truthful, honest, dignified, balanced, and economical (in line and proportion).

Would you not call the statues of Greek artists sure, precise, decisive, and real? "The Venus of Milo ... in her straight, plain folds, her hair caught back simply in a knot, no ornament of any description to set her off ... shows us how unlike what the Greeks wanted in beauty was from what the world after them has wanted."[4]

A Greek painting of a boy holding grapes was described as so life-like that "the birds flew down to peck at them, and the people acclaimed (the painter) as a master-artist. 'If I were,' he answered, 'the boy would have kept the birds away.'"[5] Miss Hamilton explains that "Grapes were to be painted to look like grapes and boys to look like boys, and the reason was that nothing could be imagined so beautiful and so significant as the real."[6] The

Greek sculptor "had no wish to alter them at all from what he saw as most beautiful: the shapes of the human beings around him."[7]

We are told, and can observe it in their literature, architecture, and statues, that the Greeks loved reason, were realists; they accepted facts, believed the real to be beautiful and that it was the mind that set all things in motion. They were analytical and reflective, valued leisure, balance, goodness, truth, simplicity, lucidity, directness, freedom, and economy. All things were examined and brought into question; the individual took responsibility for the state and was obedient only to the laws he passed himself and which he could criticize and change. There was no authoritarian church (as there was in Egypt), and no limits set on thought. The right to say what one pleased was fundamental. Only a man without fear could not be a slave.

The Greeks loved life and rejoiced in it; they loved to play, an Olympic victory being a high achievement in society. They were keenly aware of life's uncertainties and the imminence of death. Their mottos include: "Know thyself;" "Tolerance;" "See things as part of a whole, because to see things in relation to other things is to see them simply;" and "In nothing, too much."

Is this an exaggeration by the Grecophile, Edith Hamilton, of the virtues of the Periclean age? Perhaps. But, if the adjectives which describe the style of Greek literature, architecture, and sculpture are expressive of the Periclean Age worldview, then we must conclude that the classic style is a result of a distinctive or characteristic mode of thinking and feeling during that period. And if we understand that, then we will know why, when Romeo is told by Balthasar that Juliet is dead, he replies, "Is it e'en so? Then I defy you, stars." This most tragic moment of his young life is expressed so economically, so simply, so honestly, and so truthfully that it can make you weep. It is one of the few Greek moments Shakespeare ever wrote.

It is amazing how these classic qualities have represented beauty to writers throughout the ages. In *Camino Real*, Tennessee Williams has the romanticist Byron say:

I'm sailing to Athens. At least I can look up at the Acropolis, I can stand at the foot of it and look up at broken columns on the crest of a hill—if not purity, at least its recollection … I can sit quietly looking for a long, long time in absolute silence, and possibly, yes, still possibly—The old pure music will come to me again. Of course, on the other hand, I may hear only the little noise of insects in the grass.…But I am sailing to Athens! *Make voyages! Attempt them*—There's nothing else.

Romanticism

We will give only a nod to the other "isms," but we strongly recommend the first two essays on Romanticism by Morse Peckham, whom we will quote in this chapter. Romanticism is defined as denoting the principles, characteristics, or spirit of the Romantic movement in literature, emphasizing imagination, sentiment, and individualism. By the eighteenth century, this movement had become a conscious reaction against classicism, drawing on a spirit of chivalry, adventure, and wonder, plus a preoccupation with the picturesque, suggestive, and passionate in nature. Some adjectives and phrases to describe it include: fancy; capricious; the addition of "strangeness" to beauty; an elevation of things imagined with a taste for the unusual, the foreign, the unaccustomed; inspiration rather than formal canons of construction; variety rather than unity, or freedom from rules and restrictions; an idealization of the "noble savage" and a love of that which is natural rather than manmade; and a belief in the doctrine that man is essentially good and that it is society that corrupts him. In short, romanticism is a belief in the perfectibility of man. These qualities, combined with an aura of remorse and sadness, suggest the feelings and thinking of the age which resulted in its style.[8]

Realism

We will give a bit more space to the realistic style, since it is the basis of the modern theater as well as film. Realism stresses fidelity to nature or to real life, representation without idealization, and adherence to actual fact, truth, and nature, without selection in the interest of preconceived ideals. It emphasizes geographical accuracy, minutiae of detail, and, some feel, an unfortunate preoccupation with the sordid.

Science is credited as the forerunner of realistic style, which viewed people's existence and acts as determined by heredity and environment rather than free will. The attempt was to render literature a science, and for the writer to observe scientifically, using the analytical and scientific method in her search for truth. Influenced by Bernard's *Introduction to Experimental Medicine*, Zola predicted that "the modern method of universal inquiry, which is the tool our age is using so enthusiastically to open up the future," would be the mode of the future. The starting point would be "the study of temperament, and of the profound modifications of an organism subjected to the pressure of environments and circumstances."[9] In short, realism attempted to be scientifically objective, eliminating the author's point of view, which, of course, is impossible.

In 1868, Émile Zola, who contributed to the first bill of André Antoine's *Théâtre Libre,* considered the first naturalistic theater, published his preface to the second edition of his novel *Thérèse Raquin,* in which he named the many tenets of naturalism.

> my aim has been to study temperaments and not characters....I have chosen people completely dominated by their nerves and blood, without free will, drawn into each action of their lives by the inexorable laws of their physical nature. Therese and Daurent are human animals, nothing more. I have endeavored to follow these animals through the devious working of their passions, the compulsion of their instincts, and the mental unbalance resulting from a nervous crisis. The sexual adventures of my hero and heroine are the satisfaction of a need, the murder they commit a consequence of their adultery, a consequence they accept just as wolves accept the slaughter of sheep. And finally, what I have had to call their remorse really amounts to a simple organic disorder, a revolt of the nervous system when strained to breaking point. There is a complete absence of soul, I freely admit, since that is how I meant it to be.[10]

Man's existence and acts are determined by heredity and environment, and he does not have free will. Zola states that his object was "a scientific one." "Given a highly-sexed man and an unsatisfied woman," he wished to "uncover the animal side of them and see that alone ... and note down with scrupulous care the sensations and actions of these creatures." He simply applied to two living bodies "the analytical method that surgeons apply to corpses." He was in "search for truth" and was "copying life exactly and meticulously," giving a "precise analysis of the mechanism of the human being."[11]

Zola was for abolishing many conventions of the theater: exposition, denouement, intrigue; all were unnecessary. A play had to reproduce as many incidents from the actual experience as possible. He objected to wings and drops, predicted footlights would be abolished, hated "effect" acting, and especially opposed the stereotyped manner of acting taught at the French conservatoire. He insisted that costumes fit the characters rather than displaying the actresses. He and Antoine wanted normal speech, and there was a great concern in the staging for verisimilitude, so that the reproduction would be "like truth."[12]

Naturalism, Selective Realism, and Expressionism

All of the above use fidelity to nature as a basis for their selection. In naturalism, the author chooses to select as much or as many incidents from the actual experience as she possibly can; in realism, she is more selective; in selective-realism, she selects still fewer incidents in her attempt to arrive at truth.

If we were performing the nativity play in a naturalistic style, we would come as close as possible—within the necessary heightening of the actual—to reproducing a barn, such as Jesus was born in, onstage. We would leave one end open so that the audience could see the stanchions, cows and camels, hay, straw, manger, and animal dung, and above, the sky and stars. If we decided to do the production in the style of realism rather than naturalism, the designer would start to take away design elements. The first thing he would remove is the animal dung, then the cows and camels, and perhaps the hay or straw, except for just a bit around the manger. If the play was in the style of selective realism (that is, to select, let's say, four objects to represent the whole), the designer might choose a manger, the gable end of the barn hung from the flies, a single star in the background projected on the cyclorama, and a bale of hay or straw.

In expressionism, we see the leading character's subjective emotions and sensations represented. This is accomplished through the most plastic means of stagecraft: lights and sound.

The scenes that go back in time—remember they are not flashbacks[13]—in Miller's *Death of a Salesman,* originally titled *The Inside of His Head,* are also expressionistic. They are recalled from Willy's mind. When Linda's darning of her stockings reminds Willy of the woman in Boston, he first hears echo-chamber laughter, and this draws him into the scene with her. Since it is a memory taking place in the present, it can be played almost anywhere without scenery. Designer Jo Mielziner drew the audience into these memories by the use of music, light, and sound.

Architectural Style

Perhaps no one in the history of theater was more aware of the relationship between the architectural style of the theater and the given script than William Poel. The importance of his work and influence on Shakespearean production in England, at the end of the nineteenth and the beginning of the twentieth centuries, is tremendous.

Robert Speaight writes that Poel believed part of the strong popular appeal of Shakespeare's plays on the Elizabethan audience was in the "perfect adaptability of the plays to the theatre in which they were performed."[14] At a time when Sir Henry Irving and others were giving star performances in picture-stage, proscenium productions with tons of realistic scenery, costumes, sound, and lighting effects, Poel was the sole dissenter, not because he did not like the rich pictorial effects, but because he found them to be "irrelevant to the imagery of Shakespeare's plays and destructive to their rhythms."[15]

Poel advocated a return to the stark simplicity of the Elizabethan platform stage, with its intimacy (no member of the Globe Theatre audience was
more than thirty feet from the actors standing at the front of the thrust), its
nonlocalized character, its emphasis upon architecture rather than decor,
and its plasticity rather than picturization: where the actors "stood out 'in the
round' like statues" as opposed to proscenium staging, "where the actor is
flat framed in a recess."[16] Poel liked the easy flexibility of the Elizabethan
stage, where actors and audience members were under the same roof, or on
the same stage; where the audience was *in* the play, not outside; and where
the author was not subordinate to scenery and spectacle:

> Poel saw that what the Elizabethan stage, with its daylight, its multi-
> ple planes and its wide projecting platform made possible was a spe-
> cial kind of realism. The audience was *in* the play not in front of it; the
> action of the play was not Rome or Alexandria; it was here and now; it
> was Elizabethan and immediate. An Elizabethan performance was
> essentially an experiment with time. The eyes of the audience were
> never invited to desert the solid octagonal walls of the playhouse but
> their imaginations were asked to superimpose upon them the visible
> universe of the dramatist….the dramatist who knew his business was
> quick to indicate the locality in question, and thenceforward he and
> the audience between them did the scene-shifting. There was no
> effort to create illusion—that is the prerogative of the picture stage—
> but there was a mutual imaginative effort which secured that those
> actors should be Romeo and Juliet and also Elizabethan Englishmen.
> …The Elizabethan stage was a map of anywhere, and when a land-
> scape was required, the poet was at hand to paint it.[17]

The simplicity of the setting forced Poel's actors back upon the text.
The "acting editions" of the time were crusted with the barnacles of
decades of star actor's "business." Poel tried to discover what effects literal
fidelity would produce by the "startling original idea of reading the play."[18]
He maintained that the Elizabethans "were athletes, not eunuchs, of the
imagination, and when they went to the theatre they demanded the
opportunity for exercise."[19] Speaking of the "tyranny of the visual arts," Poel

"feared that the imaginative faculties of modern man—faculties essential for the enjoyment of Shakespeare—were being smothered by the insistent appeal to the eye, which at every turn was flattered … until it threatens the adult with paralysis of the imagination."[20]

Poel directly influenced not only Shakespearean production but also the style of production for many other plays. Here, then, is a prime example of the history of Shakespearean production being turned upside down because a man thought of a play in terms of the architectural style of the theater for which the play was first written. Whether or not one agrees with Poel's insights, it raises important questions for theater artists to think about when staging a Shakespeare play. What is lost by setting *Macbeth* in a realistic set? What happens if you use Baroque Italianate scenic design? It doesn't mean that you can't, or that there is only one way to stage a Shakespeare play, but whatever choices are being made should be rooted in the play itself.

Writers' Style

If we accept the proposition that a writer's style is reflective of her relationship to life, then it follows that an understanding of that style should be a major concern to anyone interested in realizing the dramas the writer has written.

Richard Boleslavsky, one of a number of Russian émigré theater artists responsible for bringing Stanislavsky's acting system to the United States, addressed this very issue. Much of his book is conducted in the form of a dialogue between the "I," representing Boleslavsky, and the "Creature," his Socratic foil. In the following exchange, Boleslavsky explains that sensitivity to the author's thought and rhythm, as revealed through his use of language, is essential for the actor in order to give true characterization:

> I: Characterization of the mind (in a role) … is largely a question of the rhythm. The rhythm of thought, I should say. It does not so much concern your character as it concerns the author of that character, the author of the play.

THE CREATURE: Do you mean to say that Ophelia should not think?

I: I would say that Shakespeare did all the thinking for her. It is his mind at work which you should characterize while acting Ophelia, or for that matter, any Shakespearean character. The same goes for any author....

THE CREATURE: I never thought of that. I always tried to think the way I imagined the character would think.

I: That is a mistake which almost every actor commits.... [T]he most powerful weapon of an author is his mind. The quality of it, the speed, alertness, depth, brilliancy. All of that counts, without regard to whether he is writing words of Caliban or those of Jeanne d'Arc, or those of Osvold. A good writer's Fool is no more foolish than his creator's mind, and a prophet no more wise than the man who conceived him. Do you remember Romeo and Juliet? Lady Capulet says about Juliet, "She's not fourteen." And then a few pages later Juliet speaks.

My bounty is as boundless as the sea,
My love as deep; the more I give to thee,
The more I have, for both are infinite.

Confucius could have said that, or Buddha, or St. Francis. If you will try acting Juliet's part in a way which characterizes her mind as a fourteen-year-old mind, you'll be lost. If you try to make her older you'll ruin Shakespeare's theatrical conception which is that of a genius. If you try to explain it by the early maturity of Italian women, by the wisdom of the Italian Renaissance, and so forth, you will be all tangled up in archaeology and history, and your inspiration will be gone. All you have to do is to grasp the characterization of Shakespeare's mind and follow it.

THE CREATURE: How would you describe the quality of it?

I: A mind of lightning-like speed. Highly concentrated, authoritative, even in moments of doubt. Spontaneous, the first thought is always the last one. Direct and outspoken . . . whatever character of Shakespeare you perform, its mind (not yours but the character's) must have those qualities in its manifestation.

THE CREATURE: Would you say the same if I had to act in a Bernard Shaw play?

I: More so in Shaw's case. His peasants, clerks and girls think like scholars, his saints and kings and bishops like lunatics and monsters. Your portrayal of Shavian character would be incomplete unless the mind of that character, embodied in its ways, contained attack defense, continued provocation for argument, right or wrong. . . . it is mostly the rhythm or organized energy of your delivery of the author's words. After studying him and rehearsing him for a length of time, you ought to know the movement of the author's thoughts. They must affect you. You must like them. Their rhythm must infect yours. Try to understand the author. Your training and nature will take care of the rest.[21]

The speed, concentration, authority, and spontaneity that Boleslavsky detects in the writing are manifest in the words themselves, and represent a characteristic mode, manner, or way of expressing an author's personal identity. To define this writing style is essentially an analytical process, not a creative one. This is precisely the reason there can be no such thing as a "dumb" artist.

An author's style of writing is described by adjectives: words used with nouns to denote a quality, something attributed to it, or the range of application of the thing named. Style is the way a writer puts words together—in phrases, sentences, paragraphs, scenes, and acts—with attention to their clarity or obscurity, brevity or long-windedness, vitality or lethargy, sincerity or irony, and their use of contrast, simile, and metaphor.

This process of analysis is not undertaken merely for its own sake, but to connect—and reflect—the style of the writing in all the architectural components and structural parts of the production so that it has unity as a whole. The following exchange between Macbeth and Lady Macbeth takes place right after Macbeth has murdered Duncan:

MACBETH: I have done the deed. Didst thou not hear a noise?

LADY MACBETH: I heard the owl scream, and the crickets cry.
                 Did not you speak?

MACBETH:	When?	
LADY MACBETH:		Now.
MACBETH:		As I descended?
LADY MACBETH:	Ay.	
MACBETH:	Hark!	
	Who lies I' the second chamber?	
LADY MACBETH:		Donalbain.
MACBETH:	This is a sorry sight	
LADY MACBETH: A foolish thought to say a sorry sight.		

What adjectives would you use to describe the writing? Breathless? Pulsing? Feverish? Suspenseful? Urgent? If you were directing a production of this play, do you think analyzing the writing in this way might help the actors to understand how the scene might best be played? Murderers, after all, undoubtedly react to their crime in a variety of ways. It's conceivable that for some the act is altogether casual. Shakespeare's Richard III coolly declares, "Why, I can smile, and murder whiles I smile" without straining audience credibility. But the style of writing here clearly suggests something else is happening with these two characters. They both seem tense, nervous, and jittery. How do we know? The style of the language tells us. Out of fifty-one words in this act, all but seven are monosyllabic. Short, sharp, stabbing words like "hark," "scream," "cry," "speak" are used by Shakespeare precisely because they fit the temper of the action.

The formatting of the lines themselves is another clue. Notice how in certain places the first word from one line comes directly after the last word in the previous line, not at the left margin, as it would normally. This is to indicate that such words are to be spoken as one continuous line, without pause, which will necessarily impart speed and urgency to the delivery. True, such formatting was the result of later emendations to the text, but it nevertheless seems utterly consistent with the dramatic need of the scene, as anyone who has ever acted it will tell you. Try acting it in front of an audience, taking long pauses between each word, and decide for yourself if this is true.

At the other end of the stylistic, Shakespearean spectrum is the modern British playwright Harold Pinter, known for his relatively sparse and elliptic dialogue. One of his most famous plays, *Betrayal*, deals with a love triangle between Emma, her husband Robert, and her lover, Robert's best friend, Jerry. The following excerpt is from act 2, scene 5.

(Hotel room. Venice. 1973. Summer. EMMA on bed reading. ROBERT at window looking out. She looks up at him, then back at the book.)

EMMA: It's Torcello tomorrow, isn't it?

ROBERT: What?

EMMA: We're going to Torcello tomorrow, aren't we?

ROBERT: Yes. That's right.

EMMA: That'll be lovely.

ROBERT: Mmn.

EMMA: I can't wait (Pause)

ROBERT: Book good?

EMMA: Mmn. Yes.

ROBERT: What is it?

EMMA: This new book. This man Spinks.

ROBERT: Oh that. Jerry was telling me about it.

EMMA: Jerry? Was he?

ROBERT: He was telling me about it at lunch last week.

EMMA: Really? Does he like it?

ROBERT: Spinks is his boy. He discovered him.

EMMA: Oh. I didn't know that.

ROBERT: Unsolicited manuscript. (Pause) You think it's good, do you?

EMMA: Yes, I do. I'm enjoying it.

Pinter takes a general characteristic of middle-class English behavior—measured, reserved, controlled speech—and forges it into a style that is almost instantly recognizable as his own. Whereas, in the scene from

Macbeth, the words tumble out breathlessly, Pinter's characters seem to be calculating the effect of each and every syllable, and choosing their words accordingly. There is something hidden—subtextual—not only in the way the characters speak to each other, but also in how the playwright speaks to us through the stage directions. The bare minimum of information is given. We know the year, the season, the city, the immediate location, and the relative positions of the bodies, and that's it.

The characters' lines seem to be as significant for what is not said as for what is, a characteristic we don't typically associate with Shakespeare's writing. In the *Macbeth* scene, for example, once one is familiar with both the context and the vocabulary, what the characters are saying relates quite clearly and directly to their actions. In the Pinter play, however, there is a disjunction between what is being said and what the characters are thinking.

The story is about the destructive synergy of a failing affair, yet these characters are talking about vacation plans, books, and some author utterly irrelevant to the plot. Clearly, something else is happening beyond the literal meaning of the words. This disassociation between words and actions, between what people are saying and what is really going on between them, is at the heart of Pinter's style. If this style is ignored, and the scene were played with the same direct, open, rapid-fire energy of the scene from *Macbeth*, something very central to the meaning of the Pinter piece would be lost or distorted.

Designers' Style

Almost everyone would agree: the granddaddy of twentieth century American stage designers was Robert Edmond Jones (1887–1954). Known as a major promoter of what was called the "new stagecraft," which consisted of innovative new theatrical trends in European scene and lighting design, Jones worked as designer for the Provincetown Players on the experimental works of Eugene O'Neill and, later, for the enormously influential Theatre Guild, whose productions were sent out on tour throughout America after their Broadway runs.

The following is from chapter 5 of Jones' legendary *The Dramatic Imagination*, which should be required reading for anyone interested in dramatic storytelling for the stage or the small and large screen.[22] In it, Jones discloses the creative process taken in designing a costume for the biblical character Delilah, as envisioned by John Milton in his poetic tragedy *Samson Agonistes*. You should note that, although he is specifically dealing with the creation of a costume, the creative journey undertaken illustrates the process of any designer for film or stage, whether for costumes, scenery, lights, sound, properties, or set dressings.

Jones deliberately chose John Milton's poetic work, modeled on Greek tragedy because, as anyone connected with show business knows, *Samson Agonistes* (1671) is so far removed from drama's mainstream as to be virtually unknown. Its periods encompass the biblical, Milton's own time, plus clothing style in America during the first forty years of the nineteenth century, when Jones was most active.

If it's set in biblical times, why would the nineteenth century be important? To answer why this is so, take a look at the episodes of HBO's *Rome* on DVD. Although the apparel worn is totally different from what we wear today—impeccably true to the Roman models—it is designed so as to reflect not only its own time but also ours, since the intention of the

---

TIME AND ETERNITY

Every work is rooted in time. And if it doesn't express the times it's written in, the anguish of its times, the problems or some part of the problems of its times, it's no good. It's no good because it has no substance or historical reality, in other words no living reality....At the same time if the characters described in a work are too closely linked to their era, they become the expressions of an inadequate, restricted humanity. Which is why all worthwhile literary works stand at the crossroads between time and eternity, at the ideal point of universality.

Claude Bonnefoy, *On Conversations with Eugene Ionesco*, trans. Jan Dawson (New York: Holt, Rinehart and Winston, 1971), 120.

series was to do just that: to highlight a comparison between the two times. Costumes—regardless of the historic period—rather than calling undo attention to the uniqueness of a specific period, usually attempt to reflect not only the historic period of the time and place of the production but also that of the present.

The topic in Jones' book is the dramatic imagination, and his point of view is that this endowment to all of us, is, by nature, "the most precious, the most powerful and *the most unused* of all human faculties." To unitize it, he believes artists must first go through a necessary apprenticeship, which consists of routine training and endless experimentation. They must know and be able to identify historic periods as well as be trained in the specific technical knowledge of patterns, farthingales, wimples, patches, etc., and have knowledge of what fabrics will look like onstage, whether in motion or repose.

Jones also speaks of the endless work and the routine involved in developing "the brains that are in the fingers," which enhances a feeling for style, and as near perfect and thorough a knowledge as the young artists can manage until "they are released from it." Then it is time to design a costume for a specific character.

The first thing to do is to read the play. Professor Emeritus Van Phillips of Purdue University apprenticed early in his career with New York designer Jo Mielziner (*Streetcar, Salesman*, etc.). Van tells the story of his advice to a graduate student directing *Marathon 33*, which Mielziner, visiting artist for a semester, said he would like to design. "Read the play over and over and over again until you really know it. Don't be caught in a situation where you are unable to answers any question, the knowledge of which is contained in the script."

As with all designers, Jones read the Milton script and came upon the following passage:

> But who is this, what thing of Sea or Land?
> Female of sex it seems,
> That so bedeckt, ornate, and gay,

Comes this way sailing
Like a stately ship
Of Tarsus, bound for th' Isles
Of Javan or Gadier
With all her bravery on, and tackle trim,
Sails fill'd, and streamers waving,
Courted by all the winds that hold them play,
An amber scent of odorous perfume
Her Harbinger.

With the "two essentials of stage costume in mind—theatricality and appropriateness," he is stimulated to visualize the costume he must design. And the beginning for inspiration is the above passage from the play, which makes him ask, why did the author create this particular character in this particular way instead of some other way?

His imagination kicks in as images—"not erudite, but evocative"—flood his mind; images that go even beyond the three historic time periods mentioned above, but nonetheless play a part in his imagination's quest for the costume:"tight bodice, full stiff skirt, ruffs, jewels. Great names rise in the memory: England's Elizabeth the Queen, who once said, 'I could have wept but that my face was made for the day'; Sir Francis Drake, the defeat of the Spanish Armada, when the streets of London all hung with blue, like the sea; Shakespeare, Kit Marlowe stabbed in the Mermaid Tavern, Sir Walter Raleigh, with his cloak and his sea knowledge and his new colony, Virginia on the other side of the world; Essex; Mary of Scotland, 'whose skin was so fair, men said, that when she drank red wine you could see the red drops running down in her throat like fire.'"

Jones calls up images that are "stirring, blood-swept, passionate," and that mingle and blend in the minds in an overpowering sense of splendor, reckless adventure, and energy as his dramatic imaginations begin to sketch the first vague outline of the costume:"fantastic, elaborate, ceremonious, splendid." He then considers the costume in relation to Milton's poetry, which he describes as "ordered, splendid, a gorgeous pageant, a concert of organ and orchestra led by a master of sound, laid out like a formal garden, all glowing in autumn sunlight, along whose enchanted avenues we may wander until the tempest comes, and the lightning splits the sky and the earth reels, and we hear the voice in heaven chanting." And the costume takes on a new quality: "more triumphant, astonishing, a certain elegant sobriety, Miltonian." He remembers that in Milton's time:

> "the old theatre lighting, in spite of its crudeness, made by hundreds of tiny tapers placed above the proscenium, had a quality of dreaminess which our modern lighting sadly lacks. And with this the figure appears, … like something seen between sleeping and waking, or in a daydream, it moves in a quivering amber twilight, a romantic dusk. In that low shadowless amber radiance the unusual, the extraordinary, the fabulous, comes into its own. Made to catch and drink up every stray wandering beam of light and reflect it back to the audience, it gleams, flashes, blazes with gold and silver spangles and jewels. Step by step it becomes clearer, becomes iridescent, becomes radiant, it glows and shines.
>
> It is Delilah, the wife of Sampson, straight out of the pages of the Old Testament, encased in an elaborate dress, so stiff it almost stands alone. It brings on childhood memories and moods; an atmosphere of nobility and betrayal and vengeance and divine justice. Now the dramatic imagination invests the costume with wonder and awe and a kind of dark glory. It is the costume for Delilah, the enchantress, to wear in her moment of triumph over the husband whom she has betrayed and blinded.
>
> Milton has compared the figure of Delilah to a ship. A stately ship of Tarsus, a galleon moving slowly, billowing folds of the stiff brocaded Oriental silks like a whispering sound, like waves breaking on the shore. There is a rippling of light and a soft rustling and a foam of lace on the purfled sleeves and a sheen of gems over all, a mirage of sapphires and moonstones and aquamarines and drops of crystal. Great triple ruffs float upon the air, and veils—'slow-dropping veils of thinnest lawn'—droop and fall with the figure's stately dippings and fillings and careening over the smooth floor of the sea.

We see it for an instance, plain and clear
Now it has vanished
We saw it!
And now we must make it.

Trust us! It's a thrilling read. If you want to know something about stage design—indeed, something of creativity itself—and the complexity and rewards of style based on a full knowledge of history, literature, and writing enhancing and inspiring the artists' dramatic imagination, you *must* read this book.

Directors' Style

It is essential to know that the director, as we know him today, was not a part of theatrical production until the end of the nineteenth century—his duties being carried out by the playwright or leading actor. The first group of theater artists to fulfill the role of what we now call the director were: Georg II, the Duke of Saxe-Meiningen (actually Ludwig Chronegk, his regisseur) noted for his spectacular antiquarian productions with attention to crowd scenes; André Antoine at the *Théâtre Libre*, noted for his slice-of-life realism in content, acting, and production; Constantin Stanislavsky at the Moscow Art Theatre, noted for his naturalistic productions with method ensemble acting; Vsevolod Meyerhold, noted for nonillusionary theatricalism with constructivist settings and physicalized acting; Max Reinhardt, noted for imaginative and spectacular Neoromanticism in non-proscenium arch settings; and William Poel, noted for productions of the Elizabethan revivalist style.

A cursory examination of the work of two twentieth-century directors, Bertold Brecht and Eliza Kazan, will suffice to illustrate director's style.

Brecht was both a writer and a director. His productions were in episodic form. As with Marlowe and Shakespeare, he created great individual roles. Prior to each scene, there was narration, directly addressed to the audience, either projected on a screen, spoken by an actor, or both. The information conveyed was a kind of scenario of the scene that followed. Thus, suspense, a keystone in conventional drama, was greatly reduced or eliminated.

There was strident or cacophonous music. The Paul Dessau score for *Mother Courage and Her Children* was played by an "orchestra" of one percussionist, one flute, one piccolo flute, one muted trumpet in C, one accordionist, one guitarist, and a piano with thumbtacks on the hammers.

As for stagecraft, Brecht used the selective realistic style for scenery. Partial set pieces (really regarded as stage properties) were used to represent the whole. Utilitarianism was stressed over so-called aesthetic qualities. As for color, if you took all colors and reduced their saturation and brilliance to the same degree that sepia has been reduced from yellow and brown, you would have the colors used in many of his settings. Light sources and orchestra members were not masked or out of sight under the stage since there was no pretense at a representational style.

The Berliner Ensemble company used a large cyclorama, not for the illusion of infinite space, but as something on which to project their slides. If a cyclorama was not available, side or overhead screens were substituted. And in the case of *The Threepenny Opera* produced at the *Schiffbauerdamm* in 1928, there was the famous half-curtain that looked like, and probably was, several bedsheets strung together on a wire. The opening of this half-curtain by the street singer was incorporated as "business" that is used today in theaters with plush velvet curtains, a good example of empty "style" where externals are used, but there is no internal reason for using them.

As for acting in epic drama, Brecht said:

> the actor should be plastic but not mannered, accomplished and subtle but not ostentatious and artificial. They should not squander all their art on the single trick of pretending to *be* the character they are portraying; or if they are actors who have been trained in the school of *Einfuhlung*—that is feeling one's way into the role and into the hearts of the audience—will have to give more of their attention to the art of *Verfremdvng*—that is setting one's self at a distance from both audience and character portrayed.[23]

In his alienation-effect (or A-effect) essay, Brecht tells us what he does *not* want acting to be. He does *not* want the actor to "generate a mood by a broken speech-rhythm"; "warm the audience up by unloosing a flood of temperament, not cast a spell over them by tightening his muscles ... or to put them in a trance"; "or to be transformed into the man he presents so that nothing of himself is left." He wants the actor to "eschew all premature 'living himself into' the role," to find an outward expression through gesture in order to convey what is going on inside, and he wants his actors to think, to make decisions, rather than acting without thinking of the alternatives; in short, to cross-down stage left because you choose not to cross-down stage right.[24]

To avoid bad acting, Brecht suggests three ways for the actor to approach a role: adapt the third person, use the past tense, and speak the stage directions and comments before the line. These are, he makes clear, rehearsal techniques, not techniques that are incorporated into the performance.

There is a Marxian dialectic in the social-economic aspect of the production's theme that is didactic and political. Mother Courage is described as a "hyena of the battlefield" and is shown haggling over business transactions at the precise moment that each of her three children is killed. Brecht is more interested in illustrating his theme than in having the audience become so involved through empathy that they do not get the message. This is why in *Theaterarbeit* he insists that his plays "be produced in the style in which he originally presented them."[25]

These, then, are some of the theatrical devices that epitomize Brechtian style. "He ... challenged the whole theory of synthesis in production"; that is, the idea of fusing all elements into an organic unity as had been suggested by Wagner and, later, Appia and Craig. Such a fusion struck Brecht "as the technical means of giving pseudo life to corrupt ideas."[26]

The point of Brecht's style is to constantly remind the audience that it is in a theater, witnessing a performance, that the audience will "assume an enquiring, critical attitude toward events" in order "to show how the world works, to the end that the world may be changed."[27] He wanted audiences to be challenged by the play and not become so involved through empathy that they could not think of alternatives to action. This is the inner reason for the *outward* mode.

None of the above, however, even remotely suggests that, in producing a Brecht play, a cerebral approach should be used. Without a vital, gut-level reason for using any particular set of conventions, the result is almost certain to be a hollow shell. Style always has a essential connection between the external and internal: the external being simply a by-product of the vital internal feeling of the primary artist toward experience. If you want to *see* what Brecht's style looked like, examine his *Couragemodell 1949*.

Elia Kazan directed thirty Broadway productions and twenty films. He was—arguably—one of the top American directors of the twentieth century, his forte being his understanding of actors, the working process, and dramatic structure. His weakness was in understanding how cinema photography can tell a story as well as plot, dialogue, or characters. Kazan left his personal stamp—his style—on everything he directed, both in the theater and in film. Unlike Brecht, he did not author the plays he directed, although in *Cat on a Hot Tin Roof*, what is usually produced as the third act includes choices that are the director's rather than the author's. In his Broadway productions and his films, he was most successful when his personal style fused with the style of the writer, as usually happened when he directed Miller or Williams.

For the most part, Kazan managed to connect his own, unique, creative force with that of an author, and this fusion was accomplished through his understanding of the acting process, whereas Brecht's strength was as an author-director. Above all else, Kazan understood acting; he was himself an excellent actor in Group Theatre productions. It is for this reason that a vital internal feeling, a life force, a kind of hypersexual energy, infused all his productions. At the same time, this energy was juxtaposed with a male softness, a sensitivity, which revealed itself in a kind of poetic naturalism. These combined qualities and their contrasts are in all the Kazan works. It is characteristic of his productions that, in one or two scenes, an orgiastic energy explodes. In addition, there is a clean, clear-cut delineation of the struggling forces and their social-economic basis, especially all through *Sweet Bird of Youth*.

In a Kazan production, there is always a reality, an honesty, and an unpredictability that is both identifiable and moving because Kazan seems to draw it in equal parts from the author's character, from himself, and from the actors with whom he is working. In many instances, the actors seem to become the characters. He appears to have deeply and permanently influenced most young actors who worked with him, such as Marlon Brando, James Dean, Paul Newman, Geraldine Page, Julie Harris, and Barbara Loden, among others.

Kazan took the 1930s Group Theatre acting style (as interpreted by Lee Strasberg, Harold Clurman, and Stella Adler) and made it uniquely his own. It lasted through the mid-1960s as the dominant style of acting in this country, and it continues to influence the art of film acting today. In addition, the actors Kazan influenced also had enormous influence on the American public. The Kazan style has been a prominent mode for at least a quarter of a century.

Actors' Style

It is interesting to note how the subject of style was viewed by the late Uta Hagen, certainly one of the great actresses and acting teachers of the twentieth century, and, perhaps, the one whose views on style are best known. In her first book, *Respect for Acting* (with Haskel Frankel), published in 1973, she devotes slightly less than two pages of a four-page chapter to style. What everyone who took an acting class from her will remember is her first pronouncement: "Style is the dirtiest word in the actor's vocabulary. It belongs to critics, essayists, and historians, and fits nowhere into the creative process. It is serviceable for catalogues and reference books. But in the act of creation, whether it be a baby or a role in a play, you cannot predetermine style (shape, sound or form)."[28]

So much for style! Case dismissed!

Whoa! Not so fast! Her second book, *A Challenge for the Actor*, published in 1991, devotes a nineteen-page chapter to style. What caused the change of emphasis in the intervening eighteen years? First, the major source of employment for professional actors came with the proliferation of the Resident Professional Theatre companies whose seasons almost always included a classic. This caused a demand for training in style. Secondly, she may have been influenced by the critical reception of her Mrs. Clandon in Shaw's *You Never Can Tell* in 1986.

She was not exactly new to plays of another time and place, having debuted in 1937 as Ophelia in *Hamlet* and, the following year, appearing as Nina in *The Seagull*. In 1943, she was Desdemona in *Othello* with Paul Robeson, followed by *St Joan* (1957), Lyubov in *The Cherry Orchard* (1968),

---

HAGEN IN *YOU NEVER CAN TELL*

Reviews of Hagen in Shaw's *You Never Can Tell*.

1) Frank Rich of the *New York Times* said:"As played by Uta Hagen, the woman is subdued, all-wise and earnestly maternal; we find no trace of Mrs. Clandon's implicit, satirically intended fatuousness (or of the ideological fire that the same actress brought to Shaw's Mrs. Warren last season). Ms. Hagen's misconceived, if smoothly executed, performance is all too in keeping with ... [this] strangely dour, laughter-smothering approach to much of the play's first half."

2) This was followed by a Sunday *New York Times* article by critic Mel Gussow: "the mother is noticeable more for her restraint than for the brilliance of her argument. This is not a role designed to show Miss Hagen to her best, most colorful advantage."

3) *New York* magazine critic John Simon wrote,"Uta Hagen, though she neither looks nor sounds right as Mrs. Clandon, manages a performance of considerable intelligence and humanity, perhaps a bit too much of the latter, the sharp haughtiness of Frieda Inescort in 1948 was more appropriate."

4) Moira Hodgson of *The Nation* says only:"Uta Hagen is strangely muted in the role of Mrs. Clandon."

5) William A. Henry III of *Time* comments:"Hagen can be one of the stage's great ripsnorting viragoes ... seems a little odd ... as a dithery, warmhearted mother who is preoccupied with her children's welfare."

6) Brendan Gill of *The New Yorker* wrote:"Uta Hagen is curiously muted as the revolutionary author, we want a Lady Macbeth, not a Mother Machree."

Frank Rich, *New York Times* (10 Oct. 1986), III, C3; Mel Gussow, *New York Times* (19 Oct.1986), II, 5.1; John Simon Theatre, *New York* (20 Oct.1986), 104; Moire Hodgson, *The Nation* (29 Nov.1986), 618–619; William A. Henry III, *Time*,"Whimsies of the Sex Wars" (26 Oct.1986), 97; and Brendan Gill, *The New Yorker* (20 Oct.1986), 100–102.

and "Vivie" Warren in *Mrs. Warren's Profession* (1985). But as Mrs. Clandon, she was—to put it as gently as possible—not exactly right. Why was this?

Throughout much of the twentieth century, style was addressed as either *representational* or *presentational*. This was the view of John Gassner, Sterling Professor of Playwriting at Yale University, in his enormously influential book *Producing the Play*, used as the basic text in colleges and universities until the 1960s. Most of Ms. Hagen's students, arriving in the city after graduating from college and anxious to keep up, were fully indoctrinated in the two styles.

Ms. Hagen adamantly opposed the presentational/representational theory and *any* teaching of style. She felt that actors too often learn to act "by imitation, by borrowing the behavior of more experienced colleagues, taking their hints about the tricks of timing ... waiting for laughs, picking up cues, simulating emotions ... from others' ready-made 'styles' for drawing room comedy as well as for slice-of-life plays." And she felt that "these conventionally accepted, easily imitated, formalistic approaches [were] passed on from generation to generation."[29]

Of representational and presentational styles, she said the terms irritated her because they were confusing (and we find her interpretations of these terms confusing). She preferred to call representational acting "formalism" and defined it as "the artist's objectively predetermining the character's actions, deliberately watching the form as he executes it." As for presentational style, she referred to it as "realism, in which the actor puts his own psyche to use to find identification with the role."[30]

Everyone connected to a production should have a uniform approach to the production's style. If we produce Ibsen's *Ghosts*, we will want to use a representational style, meaning that we wish our audience not only to believe that real things are happening to real people, but that they are also happening in a real time and a real place. To achieve such verisimilitude, the actor focuses on aspects of the character's physical, psychological, and social milieu (manners, morals, and customs of the historical period) in which the play takes place. The designers will focus on the style of architecture, clothing, set dressings, properties, plus the same issues the actor focuses on to give life to the author's characters.

If we were producing Shaw's *You Never Can Tell*, we would choose the presentational style. Again, we want the audience to believe that real things are happening to real people. But the way, manner, or mode of presentation would include less selection from the real, with a focus on the author's topic and theme. Shaw is satirizing various topics: family, the new woman, and romantic love. Mrs. Clandon's motherly concern and her humanism, although present, take a backseat to the author's satiric social comment and argument that the life force, especially love, trumps all so-called social change. He describes the character:

> Mrs. Clandon is a veteran of the Old Guard of the Women's Rights movement which had for its Bible John Stuart Mill's treatise on The Subjection of Women. She … is too militant and Agnostic to care to be mistaken for a Quaker. She therefore dresses in as businesslike a way as she can without making a guy of herself, ruling out all attempts at sex attraction and imposing respect on frivolous mankind and fashionable womankind. She belongs to the forefront of her own period (say 1860–1880) in a jealously assertive attitude of character and intellect, and in being a woman of cultivated interests rather than passionately developed personal affections. … she feels strongly about social questions and principles, not about persons.

Prior to her entrance, her two youngest children, Dolly and Philip, describe her:

> PHILIP: The fact is, Mr. Valentine, we are the children of the celebrated Mrs. Lanfrey Clandon, an authoress of great repute—in Maderia. No household is complete without her works. We came to England to get away from them. They are called the Twentieth Century Treatises.
> DOLLY: Twentieth Century Cooking.
> PHILLIP: Twentieth Century Creeds.
> DOLLY: Twentieth Century Clothing.
> PHILLIP: Twentieth Century Conduct.
> DOLLY: Twentieth Century Children.
> PHILLIP: Twentieth Century Parents.

Her first, long, revealing scene with M'Comas, her solicitor, is sample enough to reveal Shaw's emphasis of idea and the style in which the play is written:

> MRS. CLANDON: Do you go to the meetings of the dialectical Society still?
>
> M'COMAS (gravely) I do not frequent meetings now.
>
> MRS. CLANDON: Finch: I see what has happened. You have become respectable.
>
> M'COMAS: Haven't you?
>
> MRS. CLANDON: Not a bit.
>
> M'COMAS: You hold to our old opinions still?
>
> MRS. CLANDON: As firmly as ever.
>
> M'COMAS: Bless me! And you are still ready ... to insist on a married woman's right to her own separate property (she nods); to champion Darwin's view of the origin of species and John Stuart Mill's Essay on Liberty (nod); to read Huxley, Tyndal, and George Eliot (three nods); and to demand University degrees, the opening of the professions, and the parliamentary franchise for women as well as men?
>
> MRS. CLANDON (resolutely) Yes: I have not gone back one inch, and I have educated Gloria to take up my work when I must leave it. That is what has brought me back to England. . . . I suppose she will be howled at as I was; but she is prepared for that.
>
> M'COMAS: Howled at! My dear good lady: there is nothing in any of those views nowadays to prevent her marrying an archbishop. You reproached me just now for having become respectable. You were wrong: I hold to our old opinions as strongly as ever, I don't go to church; and I don't pretend I do. I call myself what I am; a Philosophic Radical standing for liberty and the rights of the individual, as I learnt to do from my master Herbert Spencer. Am I howled at? No: I'm indulged as an old fogey. I'm out of everything, because I've refused to bow the knee to Socialism.

MRS. CLANDON (shocked) Socialism!

M'COMAS:...That's what Miss Gloria will be up to her ears in before the end of the month if you let her loose here.

MRS. CLANDON: (emphatically) But I can prove to her that Socialism is a fallacy.

M'COMAS: (touchingly) It is by proving that, Mrs. Clandon, that I have lost all my young disciples. (With some bitterness) We're old fashioned:...There is only one place in all England where your opinions would still be advanced.

MRS. CLANDON: (scornfully unconvinced) The Church, perhaps?

M'COMAS: No: the theatre.

When we saw Ms. Hagen in this role, she seemed to be emphasizing the wrong mode. Her adherence to all the realistic principles she taught so brilliantly—a fidelity to the actual, an emphasis on the psychological and/or the recalling of emotions, along with the other lessons of the Stanislavsky system—was at the expense of the imagined character and situation Shaw created.

The actors must believe in the brilliant—but obviously contrived—given circumstances along with the brilliant—but obviously contrived—characters. In production, the main focus of the acting on Ms. Hagen's part—as opposed to Victor Garber, who played Valentine, and Philip Bosco, who played the Waiter, both of whom received rave reviews—was on motivation of actions, making relationships real and character creditable.

What *is* important for the mode, manner, or way of acting this play is a natural talent and enjoyment for Shaw's satiric thrusts at social conventions that both Garber and Bosco displayed. We're not sure this talent can be taught. Sure, the actor uses all the lessons learned in Acting 101 but, at the same time, stands above the character and in a humorous and lightly satiric manner comments on this *type* of "modern woman" and her intellectual beliefs. In short, the actor *presents* the audience with a typical person, one they already know as a prototype, and are amused when a mind as fine as George Bernard Shaw's takes a satiric look at her.

Conventional stage directions, such as "hold for the laughs,""pick up your cues," and "faster, louder, funnier," are, paradoxically enough, not always amiss. Shaw advised, "cues must be picked up as smartly as a ball is fielded in cricket."[31] He was writing for—and we are producing for—an audience; he is not using the play as a mounting block to expose our emotional sense memories.

Although her first book on acting is still used as the textbook in college acting classes, it is important to know that Hagen insisted, "I have disassociated myself from that book (*Respect for Acting*)."[32] Her *A Challenge for the Actor,* which took four years to write, was published five years after her appearance in *You Never Can Tell.* Could it be that her new emphasis on the topic of style reflects her critical reception in the Shaw play?

Her focus in the new book is on bringing life to a period play. Her objective is to explain how to "open the doors of the imagination, to make the past come to *life,* to find identification with the differing social mores, to be able to convince ourselves that we exist in the given world of a dramatist, the world into which he has put the play."[33] As a means to this end, she suggests paintings, travel, museums, and books to aid in the understanding and, more importantly, absorption of life.

The key word that needs understanding is that style must be characteristic (something typical, serving to identify). But, shriveling in horror, you might ask, "doesn't this lead to politically incorrect stereotyping?" To a degree, all characters are stereotypical. Why? We've mentioned this before, but it bears repetition: both film and stage are always challenged by constraints of time, and a distinctive but characteristic type is quickly recognized by an audience, preconceptions taking no time to explain. In logical discourse, one illustrates by a detailed example and then follows by specific instances that tend to prove the general case. So let us illustrate the value of the characteristic over the unique in terms of design.

Imagine the scene designer for *Gone with the Wind* in conversation with producer David Selznick. "I can prove *absolutely* that a plantation home was built in central Georgia in the 1850s in gothic style! Here's a picture of it. And I *insist* that this is my personal preference for the architectural style of Tara."

"But why do so when there was only one of that style?" Mr. Selznick asks with more than a trace of truculence in his voice, reflecting a bad day with director George Cukor. To which the designer answers by flouncing from the office.

"A bit temperamental, but an extremely talented designer," Selznick's secretary offers to soothe over the troubled waters.

"Yes, I know," Selznick replies, tight lipped. "Too bad he won't be with us after lunch!"

No, the characteristic mode of architecture at the time and place of *Gone with the Wind* was the Greek classical revival. Tara would be built in the characteristic rather than an uncharacteristic style, and if the designer felt his artistic integrity was being compromised, Selznick would find another designer! The same is often true of typecasting, whether we like it or not. We want someone unique, yes, but—for quick identification so we can get on with the plot—only unique within the characteristic type. Again, why risk losing the audience's suspension of disbelief, their poetic faith?

Do We Have Actors Who Can Act in Classical Style?

In an interview with New York casting director Stuart Howard, who has worked on a good number of Broadway and Off Broadway shows and films and commercials, who is casting director for regional theater including The Shakespeare Theatre Company of Washington, DC, and who has taught auditioning techniques at The Juilliard School and is a voting member for the Tony Awards, we asked him the following questions:

Q: Are there some actors better at playing style than others?

A: If you mean are there some actors better in plays written prior to the latter part of the nineteenth century, the answer is yes, more so now than when I started out in this business in 1975.

Q: Why is that?

A: Well, since the regional theater movement in the 1960s decentralized professional theater, actors have had more opportunities for acting in the classics. If you go through a list of shows produced on Broadway from the turn of the century to just beyond the 1960s, you will find very few classics listed. You have to remember there were more realistic plays written and produced during this time than in the previous twenty-four centuries, so actors mostly dealt with the realistic style. Freud's *Interpretation of Dreams*, published in 1900, encouraged playwrights to stress the psychological approach to character. There was also the beginning of motion pictures with 'close ups' that projected subtext and allowed the viewer to read an actor's thoughts, and, of course, there was Stanislavsky and the Moscow Art Theatre. So the problem when I first got into casting was finding actors who had a lot of experience in acting in classic plays, which obviously required a different style of acting developed during the previous centuries. The older style of acting was not only thought of as passé but actually ridiculed as ham acting.

Q: Do you think it was?

A: Coleridge said that to see Edmund Kean act was like reading Shakespeare "by flashes of lightning." There are glowing accounts of the acting of Edwin Booth, William Macready, as well as Sarah Bernhardt and Eleonora Duse (and these ladies acted in plays by Sardou and D'Annunzio, which never made the required reading list for Drama 101). But audiences obviously loved the acting of these actors as well as a whole series of others, which stretched back through David Garrick, Thomas Betterton, and Nell Gwynn. All were great bravado actors because they acted in plays that required a command of the stage, often in sweeping poetic soliloquies with either direct address to the audience or "out front" delivery of "spirit and fire"—which incidentally acknowledged them as co-creators with the writers—in what was thought of as the Age of the Actor.

Q: You mentioned Duse. Do you really think she used that kind of bravado style?

A: You're thinking of Shaw's account *The Rival Queens of the London Stage,* written in 1912, which extolled Duse's "naturalistic style" over the more theatrical style of Bernhardt?

Q: That was his point, wasn't it?

A: Of course. But is such a description of "acting style" relative? I mean is it in relation to acting styles that exist today? Or only in comparison to the acting style previous to 1912? Duse made her name in melodramatic plays by D'Annunzio, which required a larger-than-life theatrical style. So isn't it possible that toward this end she deliberately took a 180-degree opposite approach in order to come off as incredibly theatrical?

I just recently read of such an account in Arthur Miller's *On Politics and the Art of Acting*, in which he describes Jacob Ben-Ami, a great Jewish actor in the early part of the nineteenth century who was acting in a Yiddish play. One scene had become so talked about that even people who did not speak Yiddish trekked down to the Lower East Side of Manhattan just to watch this one scene. In it, Ben-Ami stood downstage, close to the audience where he put a revolver to his head and stood motionless, wide eyes with tightened jaw, sweat breaking out on his forehead, and with utter simplicity held his audience in stunned and tension-filled silence for minutes. I would call this bravura.

Q: Yes, I think I understand. Are you saying that classical plays required such style?

A: Exactly. Classical plays or, more accurately, plays written during another time and place, provided actors with such moments. And I think what we lost was much of what theater at its best is actually about—what it can provide that the big or small screen can't—and is possible only in a live performance that allows interaction between the actor and audience. This kind of theatricality depends on the actor, his personality as well as his temperament and spontaneous moods, along with his quality of voice to play the scene for the audience. In the later period, there are instances of star actors, Montgomery Clift, for example, in *The Sea Gull*, who, instead of playing to and for the audience, insisted on turning his back on them at a particular theatrical moment, possibly because his acting coach at the time said it would enable him to better feel the part.

Q: So, are you saying that style—any given style of acting—is simply being true to the play the actor is in?

A: Yes, being true to its writing, the time, and place of its given circumstances, and the period's manners, morals, customs, and conventions. Shakespeare, the French Neoclassicists, as well as all other "classical" writers, wrote their plays in what was a natural style to them. Their writing encouraged, even demanded, what we think of now as a "theatricality," which could be achieved only by actors who loved playing to the audience and, of course, this meant that they convey the lines of the play to their loyal and adoring fans even in the last row. To do so, the actor incorporated his background and knowledge in living, along with his professional experience as an actor, a resonant voice of excellent quality and range in degree of force, as well as enunciation and articulation—tongue, teeth, lips, and jaw—skills that allowed communication to a spectator of any age without shouting. This required actors not to submerge themselves in the character—"to become the character"—but to present the character, controlling and guiding all their actions and reactions. The plays required instinctive, spontaneous actors with a kind of charismatic aura, a chemistry, X factor, electricity, chutzpa, bravura—call it what you like—rebels *with* a cause, who exuded a kind of dangerous chameleon-like ability to become another—the kind of person Plato admired but would not allow in his ideal State.

Yes, there are.

We asked that he not deal with film, TV, or Broadway stars, but cite working actors—a few who are already established and the same number who are comparative newcomers. He spontaneously rattled off some twenty names, "extremely capable actors who have the talent, temperament, personality, skills, and appearance (remember the first sense we use in judging another is sight) to act in classic plays such as *King Henry V, Hamlet, Tartuffe, The Rivals, Twelfth Night, Heartbreak House, Hedda Gabler, The Green Bird, The Voysey Inheritance, Saint Joan, Uncle Vanya,* and *Ring Round the Moon* on Broadway, Off, and in major regional theaters."

In summary: All art has a style because all artists have a characteristic way of making their art. It can't be avoided. Martha Graham, the great dancer and choreographer, said, "There is a vitality, a life-force, an energy, a quickening which is translated through you into action, and because there is only one of you in all time, this expression is unique. And if you block it, it will never exist through any other medium and be lost. The world will not have it."[34]

Art reflects the artist's relationship to life experience. As she goes through life, the artist, innately sensitized to the creative possibilities these experiences hold, transforms them into artistic expressions. At some point, the exact moment is, of course, impossible to locate, there becomes a more-or-less consistent feeling toward life experience. This consistency of feeling is the foundation of an artist's style.

Notes

1. David Brooks, "The Education of Robert Kennedy," *New York Times* (26 Nov. 2006), 10 (op. ed.).

2. Edith Hamilton, *The Greek Way, The Roman Way, Two Volumes in One* (New York: Bonanza Books, 1986), 51–52.

3. Hamilton, *The Greek Way, The Roman Way*, 52.

4. Hamilton, *The Greek Way, The Roman Way*, 51.

5. Hamilton, *The Greek Way, The Roman Way*, 45.

6. Hamilton, *The Greek Way, The Roman Way*, 45–46.

7. Hamilton, *The Greek Way, The Roman Way*, 46.

8. Morse Peckham, *The Triumph of Romanticism: Collected Essays* (Columbia: University of South Carolina Press, 1970), 3–26.

9. Émile Zola, *Therese Raquin*, trans. and intro. by L. W. Tancock (Baltimore: Penguin Books, 1962), 20.

10. Zola, *Therese Raquin*, 20.

11. Zola, *Therese Raquin*, 20.

12. Zola, *Therese Raquin*, 20.

13. Arthur Miller, *Death of a Salesman, Text and Criticism*, ed. Gerald Weales (New York: The Viking Press, 167) 158–159.

14. Robert Speaight, *William Poel and the Elizabethan Revival* (London: William Heinemann, 1954), 77.

15. Speaight, *William Poel*, 77.

16. Speaight, *William Poel*, 80.

17. Speaight, *William Poel*, 119.

18. Speaight, *William Poel,* 27.

19. Speaight, *William Poel,* 57.

20. Speaight, *William Poel,* 87.

21. Richard Boleslavsky, *Acting, the First Six Lessons* (New York: Theatre Arts Books, 1933) 81–84.

22. Robert Edmund Jones, *The Dramatic Imagination* (New York: Theatre Arts Books, 1941), 95–107.

23. Eric Russell Bentley, "Bertold Brecht and His Work," *Theatre Arts* (Sept. 1944): 511.

24. Bertold Brecht, "A New Technique of Acting," trans. Eric Bentley, *Theatre Arts* (Jan. 1949): 38–40.

25. Mordecai Gorelic, "On Brechtian Acting," *The Quarterly Journal of Speech,* 60.3 (Oct. 1974): 265–278.

26. Mordecai Gorelic, "Brecht: I Am the Einstein of the New Stage Form," *Theatre Arts* (March 1957): 87.

27. Gorelic, "Brecht," 87.

28. Uta Hagen, *Respect for Acting,* with Haskel Frankel (New York: MacMillan, 1973), 216.

29. Uta Hagen, *A Challenge for the Actor* (New York: Charles Scribner's Sons), 1991: 41.

30. Hagen, *A Challenge for the Actor,* 42.

31. Bernard Shaw, "The Art of Rehearsal," originally titled "Make Them Do It Well," *Collier's Weekly* (24 June 1922), reprinted by special arrangement with Samuel French Play Publishers, page 12 in the Samuel French reprint.

32. Michael Buckley, "Stage to Screen: A Chat with Therese Rebeck: Remembering Uta Hagen," *Playbill* (18 Jan. 2004).

33. Hagen, *A Challenge for the Actor,* 215.

34. Harold Taylor, *Art and Intellect* (New York: The National Committee on Art Education for the Museum of Modern Art, 1967), 22.

Epilogue

As you might have noticed by our use of such words as evolutionary, species, mutations, and survival, one of the germinal ideas for this book was analogizing the architectural components of dramatic storytelling to Darwin's species. Evolution can benefit trees when blight thins a forest of decaying limbs and provides the remaining trees more light for photosynthesis and better growth. But misinterpreting Darwin's focus as survival of the fittest, and co-opting and skewing it with a macho spin that promotes pull-yourself-up-by-your-bootstraps competitiveness and the advantages of the free enterprise system was *not* his concern.

It took the ecological movement, popularized by *The Whole Earth Catalogue* (1968) and Rachel Carson's books *The Sea Around Us* (1951) and *Silent Spring* (1962), to draw public attention to the ravaging of the Brazilian rain forest, the melting of the polar ice cap, and the endangerment of such species as the white polar bear and the spotted owl. In fact, only at the beginning of the twenty-first century has the general public begun to understand the delicate balance of the ecosystem—the relationship *and dependence upon* organisms and their physical environment.

Remember the humpback whale in the San Francisco Bay? Entangled in so many crab trap lines, struggling to stay afloat, a fisherman alerted an environmental group who came to the rescue. At the risk of injury or even death—a single flap of her tail could have killed any of them—they worked for hours, diving and cutting the lines that entrapped her. The diver who cut the lines around her mouth said her eyes followed his every move. Free, she swam in joyous circles, and then approaching, she lovingly nudged her thanks to each of them.

If this story reveals anything, it is that knowledge of the ecosystem makes people more humane and compassionate, and this should persuade them that survival of the fittest does not address quality of life. The human species is beginning to realize that they are only one cog in this complicated interconnecting network and, as such, they are dependent on their environment and fellow species. The same is true of the various kinds of dramatic storytelling.

The standard journey for the development of a new Broadway play used to be an East Coast tryout tour plus a few previews. It depended on a delicate balance of art and commerce, consisting of comedy, serious plays, and two or three musicals per season. Now it has morphed into Las Vegas East, with a ratio of twenty-eight musicals to three straight plays at any given time during the season. Keep in mind that Broadway does not include Manhattan Theatre Club, Lincoln Center, Roundabout Theater, or other such nonprofit theater companies. If you check the Broadway listings sixty years ago, the average was thirty-plus straight plays to three or four musicals.

It is beyond the scope of this book to discuss the various reasons for this fine kettle of fish Ollie's gotten us into, but the straight play on Broadway is now an endangered species and has all but become extinct, along with old-time producers, such as Kermit Bloomgardner, Cheryl Crawford, Herman Shumlin, Robert Whitehead, and, more recently, Elizabeth McCann and Julian Schlossberg—people with intelligence and taste—to whom the straight play was what Broadway was all about.

Just because the straight play now has a much smaller audience than the Broadway musical doesn't mean that its extinction isn't going to affect the musical theater. Without *Angels in America, Born Yesterday, Death of a Salesman, Mr. Roberts, Long Day's Journey into Night, A Raisin in the Sun, A Streetcar Named Desire, The Skin of Our Teeth,* and *Who's Afraid of Virginia Woolf?* to name only a few, there wouldn't have been such musicals as *Showboat, Oklahoma, South Pacific, Gypsy,* and *West Side Story,* all of which emphasize the architectural principles of storytelling we have been discussing. One can go to a nightclub to hear songs strung together, so why go to such recent jukebox musicals as *Saturday Night Fever, The Boy from Oz, Lennon, Good Vibrations, All Shook Up, Ring of Fire, Hot Feet, The Times They Are a Changing,* and *Xanadu*—except for the scenery, costumes, special effects, music, and dancing?

But, you may ask, what about the incredible popularity of long-running musicals, which mostly eschew any plot structure, such as *Mamma Mia* and *Jersey Boys*? Today, a large percentage of the Broadway audience consists of international tourists, taking advantage of the favorable exchange rate on the dollar, who want to see a Broadway show as part of their U.S. experience. They do not speak English, but they do understand singing and dancing, spectacular costumes (especially scanty attire), special effects and scenery, which no one does better than Broadway, and so they go to the big musicals just as Americans who do not speak French go to *Folies Bergères* when they are in Paris.

Another even-larger percentage of the present Broadway audience is a young group of visitors who, having been in their high school production of *Grease* or *A Chorus Line*, want to see something familiar. And the constant revivals of the Golden Oldies, such as *Man of La Mancha*, *South Pacific, Carousel,* and *Hair*, are comfort food to the older tourists who can show how hip they still are by giving the production a standing ovation.

These out-of-towners have now thoroughly replaced a very large group of avid and perceptive theatergoers who traveled to New York yearly from every state in the union to spend a crammed week seeing all the Broadway plays they could schedule, along with a couple of musicals. Also replaced are Lower West Side Villagers and Upper West Siders who were the kind of folks who, on a warm summer evening, sat on the steps of their Brownstones talking Spinoza. This essential New York City audience no longer exists; high rents have driven them from the city—the same high rents that make it almost impossible for struggling young actors to find a place to live—just as real estate interests have destroyed some of New York's best theaters to make way for business offices.

Yet another problem is the 1978 change in copyright laws, which—disregarding the sacrosanct principle of *ex post facto*—changed copyright protection from two twenty-eight-year periods to the life of the author plus seventy years. Under the old law, a play copyrighted in 1949 was protected for twenty-eight years, at which time the author could renew the copyright for another twenty-eight years, after which the work would enter the public domain.

If this were still the case, *Death of a Salesman* or *A Streetcar Named Desire* could have been produced in 2005 without royalties because both authors were deceased. So where does the royalty money go? To a licensing agency, lawyers, playwright's agents, theaters (who contract writers "for hire"), publishers (who, having published play anthologies, can charge a fee to anyone using or quoting a play in their anthology), plus the author's heirs (who had nothing to do with the work's creation in the first place). Who instigated this change? Was it the writers or was it the barnacles and parasites who now rake in money for seventy years after the writer's death?

Does this lack of straight plays signify that, yeah, it's hasta-la-vista-baby time? We hope not because of the form is a vital and necessary connection via the food chain to both screenplay and the musical. And it is Broadway, rather than the regional theaters, that has assured universal acceptance as a place where, if you can make it there, you can make it anywhere. For if the show played the main stem, you could be certain there would be a national touring company, stock, community theater, college and university productions, and, more than likely, a film. And it would also be published for a reading public—yes, people used to *read* plays. Seeing or reading plays helped audience development and was essential for young playwrights learning the craftsmanship involved in playwriting.

The Brits (as well as the vast majority of European countries) have handled this problem extremely well, simply by subsidizing the National Theatre, the Royal Shakespeare Company, the Chichester Festival, as well as other theaters that can't compete with the more commercial productions of the West End. And this works in favor of the ecosystem of dramatic storytelling. If people can understand why their environment is affected by the melting ice cap, they should be able to understand that loss of the straight play will affect the development of the musical and dance (think Twyla Tharp *Movin' Out* and Susan Strohman's *Contact*) as well as film.

And, speaking of film, in Hollywood a similar devolution from story to glitz has occurred. Whatever the problems of the old tyrannical studio system, the studios were staffed by people knowledgeable in the story arts. Many had backgrounds in theater and literature. The stars themselves often began their careers doing straight plays on Broadway. Even in the lower budgeted, so-called B films, the work was usually rooted in coherent plot principles. And yes, many of them were awful, but not because of their coherent plots. They were awful because they were deficient in the other architectural components of a good dramatic story—original characters, insightful themes, and unique style. In short, they were bad because they were clichéd.

Now, Hollywood's emphasis seems only to be money making rather than the delicate balance of art and commerce. As a result, they so emphasize spectacle to the detriment of plot and character, which, as you know, Aristotle rated as number one and two in the six constituent parts, with spectacle the sixth. Oh, yes, occasionally a film—usually foreign or an indie—comes along that genuinely captivates us with the originality and the truth of its story, but for the most part we shell out our money ($11 in New York, at the time of this writing) to be subjected to illogical plots, computer-generated hoards of thousands (think *300*), eardrum-breaking sounds, and staccato jump-cuts so fast and furious as to make anyone with a healthy attention span nauseous.

We understand that a Broadway musical requires music and dance, just as we know—as did all the writers of great musicals—that their first requirement is a great story (think Arthur Laurence, author of the "books" for both *Gypsy* and *West Side Story*), and we know and love films that dazzle us with visual and auditory fanfare in ways the theater can't. The classic 1950s science-fiction film *The War of the Worlds* (to which we referred earlier) thrilled a generation with its pioneering special effects. As it is so often noted, no one who saw it could forget the Martian spacecraft, with bodies like manta rays and protruding heads like hooded cobras, blasting downtown Los Angeles to rubble. The sounds, the images, the technicolor—in short, the spectacle—made this film what it was. And what would *Star Wars* be without light sabers, imperial storm troopers, and the exploding death star? But this film—indeed, the best of Hollywood—also embraced the principles of dramatic architecture we have expounded in this book.

The same is true of the best television shows. Was *The Sopranos* just about mob shootings? (We anticipate the class cut-up's answer: "No, it was about the F word" and agree with the criticism of overuse.) In addition to the mob, there was also a gripping narrative about family, filled with characters locked in conflict, pursuing objectives, encountering obstacles, and taking action to overcome them, along with a point of view, a careful understanding of what reaction the director wanted from the audience as well as the period style. And where did these principles of dramatic storytelling originate? Look through any drama anthology and you'll find your answer: with the straight play.

Even in venues where straight plays *are* being done, there has been a noticeable shift away from the traditional emphasis on story architecture, particularly with regard to classical drama. Some of this is attributable to the ascendancy of the director and designer over the writer and the actor, of novel "concepts" over coherent ideas. Or maybe you see it as just the natural process of extinction, to which all species are heir; same for the regional, college and university theaters as well as New York's avant-garde venues, where straight plays (especially Shakespeare) *are* being done.

New York's Wooster Group—once forced by Arthur Miller to remove scenes from his *The Crucible* that they had incorporated, without permission, into their production of Elizabeth Le Compte's *L.S.D.*—recently staged *Hamlet*. Performed on an open stage backed by a simultaneously projected taping of Richard Burton's 1964 New York production, the actors moved and spoke their lines in imitation of the actors in the film. At times, frames were removed from the kinescope, producing a choppy, jerky effect on the screen, which they mimicked. Occasionally, an actor would drop out of character and ask the projectionist to fast forward, and they would then pick up at a point further along in the film.

Whatever else one might say about the production, it is clearly more about itself and the conceits of its director than about the story of *Hamlet*. In a production such as this, the play is being presented as an iconic artifact to be examined from a distance, rather than as an engaging story whose component parts mesh to illuminate the author's point of view.

Reaction, no doubt, was divided; some felt fulfilled, some alienated, and others somewhere in-between. While impugning the motives of others is always a risky business, we feel it is legitimate in this case to ask: Was the Wooster Group employing unconventional techniques to find new insight or were they pursuing, in Robert Lewis' colorful expression, "some smart-assed ego trip pasted on to the text?"[1] Were they mocking the Burton production or truly examining the play itself? Productions such as these are often referred to as experimental. But to experiment means to test out a hypothesis, not merely to follow one's impulses capriciously. It is entirely fair for audience members to demand, "is a hypothesis really being tested here?" and "how does the production illustrate it?"

There are clearly no unanimous answers, but Robert Lewis's question surely gets to the root of the matter. For if we start from the premise, as we have done in this book, that most dramas express coherent themes regarding human existence, then the success or failure of any dramatic production is based on the degree to which the production makes good on that promise.

Howver, not all productions of straight drama embody these kinds of departures from story coherence, nor is the Wooster production an isolated example. The last century saw the rise of so-called concept productions, particularly with classic plays, which were productions in which directors and designers imposed a vision on the play not found in a literal reading of it. A brief examination of this change is worth the diversion.

Remember that for most of Western theater's history there was no one called the director in the modern sense of the word. Yes, someone was responsible for the organizing and staging of the play, but whoever that person was, their main function was to follow the intentions of the playwright as they understood them. Even the early modernist movements in drama—symbolism, expressionism, futurism, Dadaism, and surrealism—stuck to this organizing principle even as they broke with traditional ways of seeing and representing life onstage and pioneered the exploration of the irrational and the subconscious.

If, for example, the director was staging a surrealist or expressionistic play, he (all directors back then were men) would interpret the meaning of the play based on an understanding of the aims of the author and conventions of the movement. If the director felt either the play or the conventions were false, rather than subverting them—as the Wooster Group seemed to be doing with *Hamlet*—he would probably not have associated himself with the production in the first place.

The Russian director Vsevelod Meyerhold (1874–1940) changed all this. Up until Meyerhold, the director was expected to stage what the playwright wrote, as literally as possible. Indeed, for most of theater history, the playwright played this role himself, which seemed natural enough, since who knew the workings of the play better than the person who created it? It should be understood, of course, that even with the utmost fidelity to an author's intentions that no two productions are ever the same. Every production is different in direct proportion to the differences of the artists working on it. The difference between Burton's Hamlet and the Hamlet of Ralph Fines will be in direct proportion to the differences between the two actors. Mechanically exact imitation is impossible.

In Meyerhold's production of Ibsen's *Hedda Gabler* (1906), there was no attempt to follow authorial intention. The director, who had been an actor under the direction of Stanislavsky, placed himself in the role of co-creator by creating afresh each character with the following result: "Each ... was allotted his own symbolic colour to match his mood and inner nature, Tesman in dull grey, Hedda in green, and so on, and each had a characteristic pose to which he returned. As the central character, Hedda also had a huge white armchair like a throne to which she withdrew."[2] None of these choices are contained in Ibsen's stage directions for the play.

Pavel Yartsev, the assistant director of the production, described how Meyerhold also broke with the realistic acting style practiced in the Moscow Art Theatre under Stanislavsky and was the style Ibsen intended.

> Realistically speaking, it is inconceivable that Hedda and Lovborg should play the scene in this manner, that any two real, living people should ever converse like this. The spectator hears the lines as though

they were addressed directly at him; before him the whole time he sees the faces of Hedda and Lovborg, observes the slightest change of expression; behind the monotonous dialogue he senses the concealed inner dialogue of presentiments and emotions which are incapable of expression in mere words.[3]

"Mere words"? Yes. Words, the means that playwrights had always used to tell the story, would now become secondary—a mounting block only—to the creation by the director who would use actions and other means to express the truth that words were incapable of revealing.

We don't intend to debate the success or failure of such an approach to any play. We didn't see Meyerhold's production, and, even if we had, we might disagree among ourselves as to its effectiveness. As for Meyerhold, perhaps he was in youthful rebellion against Stanislavsky, or perhaps he felt he was using Ibsen's play to create some entirely new hybrid, or perhaps he felt he was staying true to the author's intent through his own, revolutionary means. Whatever he felt, his directorial innovation had, over time, a growing and profound impact on the way directors in the West thought about their relationship to the play and the intentions of the author.

Of course, what Ibsen himself may have thought about this new style of directing is an open question; we can only presume there was no causal relationship between Meyerhold's production and the playwright's death from a heart attack the same year!

The last part of the twentieth century witnessed further rifts between the intention of the playwright and the vision of the director, as well as a deeper rejection on the director's part of narrative coherence and the unity of architectural components and structural parts. A new term, *postmodernism*, came into usage to describe these phenomena. Although this word has different meanings depending on who is using it, one central component of postmodernism is the idea that culture, and the arts specifically, has gone beyond the discrete divisions and categories that defined the modernist era.

Some postmodernists feel there is no one "ism" that can define a writer's work or the parameters in which one should strive to create. Indeed, most feel free to interpret without any link to the source material other than their own responses to it. Many tend to borrow liberally from a variety of artistic sources and media, arranging them in ways that may or may not have any coherent connection. Unity, plot, character, and theme are not uppermost; rather, the emphasis is placed on tearing apart the connective tissue between these elements in the hope—again presumably—that such a process will produce new insights. A new term came to describe this development: *deconstructionism*.

Many postmodernists also reject the proposition that there is any pre-determined logic, either structurally or thematically, to a given work. They favor, instead, the idea that every artist is free to assign her own meaning as she sees fit, since the author is only one person in the chain of

DECONSTRUCTIONISM

According to the *American Heritage Dictionary*, deconstructionism is: A philosophical movement and theory of literary criticism that questions traditional assumptions about certainty, identity, and truth, asserts that words can only refer to other words, and attempts to demonstrate how statements about any text subvert their own meanings: "In deconstruction, the critic claims there is no meaning to be found in the actual text, but only in the various, often mutually irreconcilable, 'virtual texts' *constructed by readers in their search for meaning'* (Rebecca Goldstein)."

Did you get all that? Good, because neither did we. The term deconstructionism, coined by French philosopher Jacques Derrida, has, like the term postmodernism, confused as many as it has enlightened. Derrida himself refused to give a succinct definition. In popular usage among practitioners of drama, it has come to mean productions in which the literal meaning of a play (which these practitioners deny exists in the first place) is subverted or reconfigured—deconstructed—with the aim of discovering hidden meanings, meanings that might ultimately have little to do with the conscious intention of the author.

American Heritage Dictionary, 485.

creativity, examining the text via the colliding and playing off of various conventions and styles against or in contrast to one another. This approach has often been called *pastiche*, a word defined as an artistic work consisting of a medley of pieces taken from various sources.

Richard Schechner's 1997 New York production of Chekhov's *The Three Sisters* put many of these principles into practice. Co-author of this book, David Letwin, not only acted in this production, as well as others directed by Schechner, but observed all rehearsals. Each of the play's four acts was set in a different time period, with corresponding acting and design conventions. The first act was done as if at the Moscow Art Theater in Chekhov's time, the second act in the style of Meyerhold's biomechanics, the third as if presented in a Soviet gulag circa 1950, and the last act, on microphones as if in a present-day radio studio.

To call Schechner's production a concept production is, in one sense, misleading. Every script must be interpreted, and every interpretation is based on one concept or another. If you choose to direct *The Three Sisters*

BIOMECHANICS

Biomechanics referred primarily to Meyerhold's approach to acting, intended to create a style appropriate to the machine age. His performers were trained in gymnastics, circus movement, and ballet in order to make them as efficient as machines in carrying out an assignment received from the outside. Basically what Meyerhold had in mind is a variation of the James-Lang theory: particular patterns of muscular activity elicit particular emotions. Consequently, actors, to arouse within themselves or the audience a desired emotional response, need only to enact an appropriate kinetic pattern. Thus Meyerhold sought to replace Stanislavsky's emphasis on internal motivation with one on physical and emotional reflexes. To create a feeling of exuberant joy in both performer and audience, Meyerhold thought it more efficient for actors to plummet down a slide, swing on a trapeze, or turn a somersault than to restrict themselves to behavior considered appropriate by traditional social standards.

Oscar G. Brockett, *History of The Theatre,* 5th ed. (Allyn and Bacon, 1987), 615–616.

in a naturalistic style with great fealty to the intentions of the playwright, that is no less of a concept—a thought or notion—than Schechner's approach to the play.

Jonathan Miller, the English stage director, has eloquently argued against the idea that there is a speculative or theoretical—platonic— ideal of every classic play, and that it is the job of the director to locate that ideal and correctly place it onstage without damaging its true and fixed meaning.

> In a sense, one of the measures of a great play is that it has the capacity to generate an almost infinite series of unforeseeable inflections. Had Shakespeare, by virtue of some sort of notational resource as yet undiscovered, been able to write down all these things he would have pre-empted the possibility of this successive enrichment which occurs from one performance to the next. One of the reasons why Shakespeare continues to be performed is not that there is a central realizable intention in each play that we still continue to value, but because we are still looking for the possibility of unforeseen meanings.[4]

To that end, even Jonathan Miller concedes that directors can take interpretation in manifestly abusive directions:

> Although I sponsor the idea that the afterlife of a play is a process of emergent evolution, during which meanings and emphases develop that might not have been apparent at the time of writing, even to the author, this does not imply that the text is a Rorschach inkblot into whose indeterminate outlines the director can project whatever he wants.[5]

The implication is clear: Drama, unlike an inkblot, is bound by determinate outlines—architectural components and structural parts—that help shape our responses to, and understanding of, the work's architecture organically contained within. How are we to determine, though, when a production is fundamentally violating the architectural integrity of its source material? Miller offers the assurance that it is "usually easy to identify" such violations.[6] To this end, he compares interpretations of a script with the distortions produced by various map projections. Geographical features may be squashed or elongated, but as long as they bear an identifiable relationship to the world, we understand their purpose. Fine and good, but stretch those features too far, and will we perceive the map as an image of what it purports to represent? Or will the original become incoherent?

Despite what Miller says, the problem here is the tipping point—overturning one intention into another—from clarity to chaos is *not* always easy to locate and identify, and is, indeed, highly subjective. This is particularly true in the arts.

Experimental productions, seeking by their nature to challenge audience expectations, provoke a wide range of subjective responses. What matters most is not the experimentation, but the *motive*, and in that regard, Tennessee Williams, as he so often did, said it best: "All . . . unconventional techniques in drama have only one valid aim, and that is a closer approach to truth."[7] Each spectator must decide for herself whether any particular production is living up to that standard.

*   *   *

If the architecture of dramatic storytelling we have described in this book, which has existed in Western thought and civilization since its beginnings, is to pass on its DNA, if this form of storytelling is to compete in the genetic battle of the dramatic species, artists and audiences must stand up for it as we would the spotted owl or the giant redwood. We must display the same kind of courage as was shown in 1982 when, in the face of imminent destruction of the almost perfect (for viewing and hearing) Broadway houses the Morosco and adjoining Helen Hayes, actors and at least one producer faced the bulldozers and wrecking balls. The *quid pro quo* arrangement for the demolition was that the Marriott Marquis would include a Broadway-type theater in their hotel. They did—one of the largest and worst theaters for viewing and hearing in New York City. So beware of *quid pro quo*.

"UNCONVENTIONAL DIRECTOR SETS SHAKESPEARE PLAY IN TIME, PLACE SHAKESPEARE INTENDED"

MORRISTOWN, NJ—In an innovative, tradition-defying rethinking of one of the greatest comedies in the English language, Morristown Community Players director Kevin Hiles announced Monday his bold intention to set his theater's production of William Shakespeare's *The Merchant of Venice* in 16th-century Venice.

"I know when most people hear *The Merchant of Venice*, they think 1960s Las Vegas, a high-powered Manhattan stock brokerage, or an 18th-century Georgia slave plantation, but I think it's high time to shake things up a bit," Hiles said. "The great thing about Shakespeare is that the themes in his plays are so universal that they can be adapted to just about any time and place."

According to Hiles, everything in the production will be adapted to the unconventional setting. Swords will replace guns, ducats will be used instead of the American dollar or Japanese yen, and costumes, such as Shylock's customary pinstripe suit, general's uniform, or nudity, will be replaced by garb of the kind worn by Jewish moneylenders of the Italian Renaissance.

"Audiences may be taken aback initially by the lack of Creole accents," Hiles said. "But I think if they pay close enough attention, they'll recognize that all the metaphors, similes, and puns remain firmly intact, maybe even more so, in the Elizabethan dialect."

Added Hiles: "After all, a pound of flesh is a pound of flesh, whether you're trying to woo a lady in 16th-century Europe, or you're a high school senior trying to impress your girlfriend with a limo ride to the prom, like in the last *Merchant* production MCP did in '95."

Though Hiles, 48, is a veteran regional theater director with extensive Shakespeare experience, he said he has never taken such an unconventional departure. The Community Player's 1999 production of *Othello* was set during the first Gulf War, 2001, *The Tempest* took place on a canoe near the Bermuda Triangle, and last year's stripped-down, post-apocalyptic version of *Hamlet* presented the tragedy in the year 3057. Hiles said he became drawn to the prospect of setting the play in such an unorthodox locale while casually rereading the play early last year. He noticed that Venice was mentioned several times in the text, not only in character dialogue, but also in italics just before the first character speaks. After doing some additional research, Hiles also learned that 16th-century Europe was a troubled and tumultuous region plagued by a great intolerance toward Jews, an historic context which could serve as the social backdrop for the play's central conflict.

Even the names just sort of fell into place, said Hiles, who had been planning to center the play around an al-Qaeda terrorist cell before going with an avant-garde take. "Theater is about taking risks, and I'm really excited to meet this newest challenge."

Some of Hiles' actors, however, have reacted negatively to his decision. Some are worried Hiles lacks the knowledge and talent to pull off the radical revisionist interpretation, while others characterized it as self-indulgent.

"I guess it's the director's dramatic license to put his own personal spin on the play he is directing, but this is a little over-the-top," said Stacey Silverman, who played Nurse Brutus in Hiles' 2003 all-female version of *Julius Caesar*. "I just think Portia not being an aviatrix does a tremendous disservice to the playwright. You just don't mess with a classic."

"Unconventional Director Sets Shakespeare Play in Time, Place Shakespeare Intended," *The Onion* (2 June 2007), www.theonion.com/content/news/unconventional_director_sets.

Broadway musicals, Hollywood blockbusters, and the avant garde form a part of the genetic mosaic, but biodiversity is necessary for survival. Too much of one species, and the environment's balance is disrupted. When all we have is spectacle and strung-together music for musicals, dramatic storytelling is going into decline, and "When storytelling goes bad," writes McKee, "the result is decadence."[8]

The solution to the survival of the straight play is to buy the Belasco, along with five of Broadway's smaller venues, at fair market value by the only party that would not be motivated by profit, the U.S. government; give landmark status; and do the same for other theaters across this great country. These theaters, charging a nominal price for admission, would produce the straight play, new or classic, with first-rate acting and design talent receiving a living salary. The whole national theater movement would be managed by theater lovers and professionals, such as Todd Haimes, Andre Bishop, Bernard Gersten, James Houghton, Gordon Davidson, Emily Mann, Jack O'Brien, Michael Kahn, Robert Falls, and George C. Wolfe (or any of the dozens of talented producer types we have left out). Production costs would be subsidized, and plays would have a limited—perhaps six months—run in order to free the theaters for the next production. The shorter run would attract major talent from both Broadway and Hollywood. Isn't this what the Rockefeller Panel Report members meant when they wrote, "the arts are not for a privileged few but for the many, that their place is not on the periphery of society, but at its center, that they are not just a form of recreation *but are of central importance to our well being and happiness?*"9

We can't reverse history's clock and suddenly expect the same Broadway that gave us *Streetcar* or *Salesman*. Nor can we—nor should we—demand that plays be staged and interpreted according to some fixed set of standards. All we can do is commit ourselves to the unrelenting search for what is honest and real in drama, commit ourselves to Williams' closer approach to the truth. In this journey, we must not be taken in by the superficial, the trite, or the phony, whether it rears its head in the glitziest Broadway house, the newest multiplex cinema, or the seediest off-off Broadway black box.

As part of this search, we encourage the reader to return to the roots of dramatic storytelling and rediscover, with a shock of recognition, drama's component parts for their vital connection to everyday human experience; plot, character, theme, genre, and style are as much about real human actions as they are about the art forms of plays or films.

And yet, for all that, what we write, we write on paper, not stone. And not only do we accept challenges to our premises, we also encourage them. And why not? The three of us often disagreed among ourselves ("You think the crisis of *Jaws* is *what*?!"), changed our minds countless times over, and then changed them again. The book was as much a journey through our own understanding of the architecture of drama as it was an attempt to clarify the subject to others.

When we speak of architecture, most of us think of something palpable, physical, or tactile, such as a building or a bridge. But the architecture of drama, although not something that can be reached out and touched, is no less real. Indeed, if we are to believe Plato, ideas are truly the only permanent things in life. Buildings eventually crumble into ruins, but the principles upon which they are constructed remain. In the same way, specific productions of *Hamlet*—some celebrated, some reviled, some conventional, others experimental—pass into memory, but the principles of story architecture upon which the play, musical, or film rests will endure— if we value them—lighting the way for future artists and audiences.

Notes

1. Robert Lewis, *Slings and Arrows, Theatre in My Life* (New York: Stein and Day Publishers), 122–123.

2. J. L. Styan, *Modern Drama in Theory and Practice* (Cambridge: Cambridge University Press, 1981), 78–79.

3. Styan, *Modern Drama in Theory and Practice*, 79.

4. Jonathan Miller, *Subsequent Performances* (New York: Viking Penguin, 1986), 34–35.

5. Miller, *Subsequent Performances*, 35.

6. Miller, *Subsequent Performances*, 35–36.

7. Tennessee Williams, *Tennessee Williams Plays 1937–1955.* (New York: The Library of America, 2000), 395. Mel Gussow and Kenneth Holdich selected the contents and wrote the notes for this volume.

8. Robert McKee, *Story: Substance, Structure, Style and Principles of Screenwriting* (London: Methuen Publishing, 1999), 13.

9. Rockefeller Panel Report, *The Performing Arts, Problems and Prospects* (New York: McGraw-Hill Book Company, 1965), 11.

Index

About the Authors

David Letwin

David Letwin currently teaches theater history, dramatic structure, and script analysis for actors at the Mason Gross School of the Arts at Rutgers University. He has also taught acting at Brooklyn College, Fordham University, and the New York Film Academy. He's a graduate of the SUNY Purchase BFA acting program and the MFA playwriting program at Mason Gross. David has acted and directed in New York, and was a founding member of Richard Schechner's East Coast Artists theater company. He would like to extend his deep thanks to Joe and Robin for giving him the opportunity to contribute to this book, as well as for putting up with his relentless search for the perfect sentence.

Joe and Robin Stockdale

Married sixty years, Joe's accomplishments are also Robin's: five kids (book-end girls and three boys in between); BFA, MA, PhD; Professor (and Dean) Emeritus of Theatre and Film, School of the Arts, SUNY-Purchase (sixteen years); Professor of Theatre, Purdue University (twenty-five) years and artistic director of the LORT Purdue Professional Theatre Company; director of 140 shows—half with AEA actors—including Academy and Tony award winner Anne Revere, James Earl Jones, and Frances Farmer; artistic director of the Woodstock (NY) Summer Theatre for seven seasons; directed Off-Broadway at The York Theatre Company; contributing writer for *TheaterWeek* and published in *Dramatist*, *Equity*, and *Playbill*. A story for *Argosy* got him a "distinctive short story, American fiction 1954" award; author of plays *Special Effects*, *April East*, and *Taking Tennessee To Hart*, which received New York readings and regional productions; wrote the book *Man in the Spangled Pants*, the fifty-year history of The Barn Theatre in Augusta, Michigan (published in 2000).

Robin worked for the *Pawling* (NY) *News Chronicle* (Ganett Publishers) as office manager and columnist. Robin and Joe both acted singularly and together in many shows, her best being Billy Dawn in *Born Yesterday* with the Carolina Playmakers and Hannah in *The Night of the Iguana* at Purdue. Joe acted in some sixty productions, appeared briefly in Larry Cohen's film *The Stuff*, three national commercials, and the A&E biography "Frances Farmer: Paradise Lost."

Joe was an official observer, second season, at the Repertory Theatre of Lincoln Center for the Performing Arts; official observer at the Actors Studio under Lee Strasberg; on the National Screening Committee for the Fulbright Awards; a member of the Theatre judging panel, National Endowment for the Advancement of the Arts; and visiting professor at Williams College, East Carolina University, and University of Southern California, Santa Barbara.

A grant by the Purdue Research Foundation allowed Joe to travel to the USSR, Poland, East and West Germany, England, and Ireland to visit theatres; a grant from the U.S. Office of Education took him to India to participate in a two and a half month-long seminar on music, dance, and drama. A scholarship endowment was named in his honor at Purdue, where he received the Excellence in Teaching Award from the School of Humanities, Social Science, and Education, and earned Purdue a national Samuel French Award for excellence in playwriting instruction. He is a member of the Society of Stage Directors & Choreographers, and the Actors' Equity and Dramatists Guild.

Retired, Robin and Joe live in Kalamazoo, Michigan, have six grandsons and one great-granddaughter, and were thrilled to work with the talented and extremely intelligent David Letwin, who kept them on their toes and off the street during the two years working on this project.